TWO WOMEN LIVING TOGETHER

여자 둘이
잘살고 있습니다!

TWO WOMEN
LIVING TOGETHER

Kim Hana and Hwang Sunwoo

TRANSLATED BY GENE PNG

doubleday

TRANSWORLD PUBLISHERS

UK | USA | Canada | Ireland | Australia
India | New Zealand | South Africa

Transworld is part of the Penguin Random House group of companies
whose addresses can be found at global.penguinrandomhouse.com.

Penguin Random House UK, One Embassy Gardens,
8 Viaduct Gardens, London SW11 7BW

penguin.co.uk

Penguin
Random House
UK

First published in Great Britain in 2026 by Doubleday
an imprint of Transworld Publishers

001

This edition is published by arrangement with Munhakdongne
through BC Agency, Seoul and Mulcahy Sweeney Associates Ltd

This book is published with the support of the Literature Translation
Institute of Korea (LTI Korea)

The moral right of the authors has been asserted

Illustrations by Alexis Seabrook

Typeset in 11.25/17pt Mercury Text G1 by
Six Red Marbles UK, Thetford, Norfolk
Printed and bound in Great Britain by Clays Ltd, Elcograf S.p.A.

The authorized representative in the EEA is Penguin Random House
Ireland, Morrison Chambers, 32 Nassau Street, Dublin D02 YH68.

A CIP catalogue record for this book is available from the British Library

ISBN: 9781529959567

To all the molecular families of the world.

CONTENTS

HAKU

TIGGER

CAST
(W_2C_4)

SUNWOO

HANA

GORO

YOUNGBAE

THE BIRTH OF A
MOLECULAR FAMILY

Hana   'Living alone suits me' – I think that's something only people who've lived alone for ten years straight can say. At first, I really, really loved living alone. I've lived with friends before, but dealing with conflicting personalities and habits can be quite stressful, especially when you're sharing a tight space. Having my own place where I had the last – and only – say on where to put the bathmat, how to do the laundry or arrange the books was the perfect living arrangement for me (or so I thought). A decade on, however, I was faced with a new type of stress, one that had been lying dormant. One morning in my parents' home in Busan, a four-hour drive from where I live in Seoul, I was awoken by the clinking of bowls and the soft gurgling of something my parents had got up early to concoct for breakfast. As I lay in bed taking in the sounds and aroma of rice and stew, warmth percolated in me. Perhaps that heightened sensitivity was the natural result of years of waking up to cold silence. After that morning, I suddenly became aware of the demands and efforts of living alone. Without realizing, I'd been expending energy on late-night thoughts and needless worrying. I wondered: *Was my weariness a sign that I'd grown out of the perks of living alone?*

Marriage wasn't a solution. In fact, it felt like the most foolish thing to do – running straight into another draining world, one ruled by the institution of marriage, in-laws and patriarchy. Besides, it didn't seem like any man was going to sweep me off my feet and turn me into a fool anytime soon – and that wasn't something I wanted anyway. I naturally began to seek out a different way of life. I looked into everything from living with friends to house-shares and eventually ended up meeting a woman who was very similar to me. We were both from Busan, had lived alone for a very long time, were seeking a new form of companionship that didn't involve getting a husband and we each had two cats. With some help from the bank, we bought a spacious apartment to live in together. Rather than having two separate homes where each kitchen, bathroom and hall would be jam-packed into little more than 33m², sharing one home that was twice the size and furnished with the same amenities made so much more sense. Talk about extra space! Our cats finally had the freedom to run around. Most importantly, we got a bathtub. It wasn't something I'd desperately wanted in the past – given the lack of space – but it's certainly nice to have.

It's been over two years since I started living with my cohabitant and I couldn't be happier with our arrangement. We've got our chore distribution down to a T: Sunwoo takes care of the cooking and tidying, and puts the laundry in the washing machine, while I do the dishes and cleaning, and put away the laundry. When I'm in bed, sensing another person's presence in the house instantly relaxes me. Every morning, we're woken gently by signs of this shared life, while our little greetings (*Did you sleep well? You're home! I'll be right back!*) add a splash of colour to our daily lives. When I lived alone, I had to make a conscious effort to keep up my 'emotional temperature'. But with Sunwoo around, that comes naturally. And if I ever need to raise my actual body temperature, I've got a tub to soak in.

But the best part is, we're both single. During the holidays, we'll visit our parents or ask after them. Our parents are quite pleased with our living arrangement; they find it reassuring. Sunwoo's mum always sends a box of all my favourite side dishes, and that's without me having to travel to visit them out of a sense of filial piety, as would be the case with in-laws. All I have to do is say, 'Yum!' The lightness of being single and the benefits of living with a cohabitant go hand in hand. Of course, we're lucky that we complement each other in so many ways. If either one of us had been convinced that living alone or getting married was the only answer, we would've missed out on this felicitous arrangement. Now, wouldn't that be sad?

They say that single-person households make up 27 per cent of households in South Korea. I think of single-person households as atoms. It's fully possible to lead a happy life alone. But once we reach a certain threshold, what's stopping the individual atoms from joining forces to form a molecule? A molecule can be made up of two, three, four, or perhaps even twelve atoms. Its bond could be strong or weak. We live in a generation where the most common molecule consists of a firmly bonded woman and man. But in the future, we might see a more diverse range of configurations. For instance, in this house, we're W_2C_4 – two women and four cats. And as of now, I'd venture we're a very stable configuration.

SOMEONE WHO'S REACHED THE ULTIMATE LEVEL OF ALONENESS

Sunwoo I once came across a viral article about the many levels of 'honbab', a portmanteau of the words 'honja' ('alone') and 'bab' ('meal'), meaning to eat alone. For instance, having a cup of instant ramen in a convenience store and eating a full meal at a family restaurant are two different levels of honbab. As someone who'd always eaten alone, I was fascinated. Any foodie who'd spent over twenty years living alone would become adept at enjoying their meals, with or without a meal buddy. It's like how kids whose tantrums are ignored are forced to grow up quicker. Whether it's getting off your arse to cook or going out to eat, once hunger and greed win out, and once you tune out the nosy stares, you'll find that eating alone is surprisingly easy.

I can trace my first significant honbab memory

back to autumn of my senior year in university. I'd just returned to campus after interviewing at a conglomerate and, while I was hungry, what I needed more was something good to lift my spirits.

I was caught between ruminating on the answers I should've given at the interview and agonizing over my failure to better hide my nervousness. I knew I wouldn't be getting a callback. My legs turned to jelly at the mere thought of my hazy future, which was sure to be full of many more such hurdles and defeats. I was drained, as if I'd been given a concentrated taste of the physical and mental exhaustion awaiting me once I stepped into the workforce. That day, clutching the envelope containing the money I'd received for taking part in the interview, I took myself to a pork rib restaurant.

Single diner or not, ordering two portions of meat is basic courtesy to the grill. People who live alone seldom have fresh veggies in their diet, so I diligently wrapped each piece of meat in a slice of lettuce and had doenjang stew and rice on the side. Instead of beef, which would've had me scrambling to keep the meat from overcooking, I ordered pork, so I could enjoy my dinner at a leisurely pace. I gobbled everything up, not only because it was delicious, but because my deflated ego was in serious need of collagen. Just as

I'd expected, I didn't get the job. I did, however, gain a few other things – the realization that I should eat well whenever my body and soul needed a pick-me-up; the confidence that allowed me to walk into any restaurant and demolish two servings of meat on my own; and the ability to swallow and digest tiny failures. I must've done a good job at refuelling my soul, because not long after, I landed a job that suited me far better than the conglomerate. Once I started work, there were company dinners to attend and times when those of us who'd worked overtime would go for a late dinner. Honbab then became more sacred to me, a time when I could enjoy my meals in peace and quiet.

Travelling alone is a few notches above even the highest level of honbab. In addition to eating alone, you have to plan your own route, get around, make decisions and deal with said decisions with no one else to consult. Whenever my friends were too busy, I'd go on trips by myself. Slowly, I became a pro at being alone. I quite enjoyed the rush of making decisions on the move – *Which museum should I see? Which tourist spots to skip? Should I take the straight road to get there quicker, or the seaside road for the view?* At some point I started to believe that aloneness resembled order – efficient, comfortable, beautiful.

Four years ago, I signed up for surfing lessons. Since

I had two vacation days, I decided to visit the highly recommended Jukdo Beach in Yangyang, a coastal town two hours from Seoul. I booked a short stay and lessons at a surf shop that doubled as a guesthouse and hopped in my car. The new season that had yet to reach Seoul had already arrived in Hangyeryeong Pass, and the roads glowed with the lustre of late summer and early autumn. Along the way, I pulled over whenever and wherever I wanted to take in the vistas. But there was no one to share them with. No one there to hear me talk about how much fun my new hobby was, how I had to try all sorts of funny poses to get in and out of my rubbery swimsuit, how being surrounded by tanned surfers made me feel like I was in a foreign country, how exciting all these new adventures were. My surfboard towered over me, and constantly going out into the water to wait for a wave with my ankle chained to the heavy board wore me out. Whenever a wave approached, I'd start paddling towards it, quickly rise to my feet and find my balance. Inevitably, there were many times when I fell face-first into the water. But in the instances where I took off successfully and was smoothly delivered to shore, oh, what a thrill! I'd tried snowboarding and water skiing, but surfing was a different type of fun that played on the gravity of waves and the water's texture. That rush of delight explained why I reached for my giant board again and again, running out into the sea, waiting for the next wave.

After every lesson, I *had* to have raw fish. I was on the east coast, after all. Most places didn't have courses for single diners, and so it always took a few calls before I could get a reservation. I would drive to a restaurant, indulge in seafood and return to the guesthouse. Since there was no one else to take the wheel, I couldn't pair my meal with alcohol. Everything went perfectly according to plan, and before I knew it, I was returning to Seoul with three days' worth of new, fulfilling experiences. Every moment of wonder was solely mine to savour. I even found satisfaction in overcoming despair alone, but at the end of the trip, I thought ... *Enough*. Though I'd done everything on my own – especially those things that supposedly cannot be done alone – and had become an expert at being alone, it was only a matter of time until I accepted the fact that some things were best enjoyed with other people around.

In the movie *Paris Can Wait*, Diane Lane's character is unexpectedly partnered up with a French man who has a penchant for dilly-dallying and impromptu activities. He insists on spreading out a picnic mat wherever there's a view and pairing food with good wine even if it means they can't drive later. While she is irked by her companion's dawdling, without him, she wouldn't have discovered new roads leading to the most beautiful sights. If the characters had taken the quickest route and stuck with it, the movie would've ended as soon as it started. Instead, it is thanks to her spontaneous companion that her trip becomes sprinkled with detours, relaxing breaks and unexpected events that make for a full and satisfying plot.

After reaching the apex of solitude during my solo surfing trip, I began my slow descent down the mountain I'd scaled alone and started spending more time with friends. That year, I went on a ten-day trip to Japan with two friends, and in the winter of the following year, I moved in with Hana. I still enjoy my meals alone, and I love the simplicity and ease of travelling alone. But here's what I've come to believe: the things I do alone, I remember, but the things I do with others become memories. For too long I've swallowed every exclamation, grumbled complaint and monologue. Now I think I'd like to let them out.

WHAT IF IT'S HER?

Hana   The first time I heard Hwang Sunwoo's name was in 2010. I'd just returned from a holiday in South America and had got addicted to Twitter, now known as X. On my quest for finding interesting people to follow, a few mutuals recommended I check out Hwang Sunwoo, editor of fashion magazine *W Korea*. Her handle was @bestrongnow (which many people read as 'best rong now'). I liked that she wrote a lot about what it meant to be a strong woman, so I followed her. Turns out she was clued up on a wide range of topics. But what I loved most was the witty, hilarious way that she conveyed her opinions. Her pieces for *W Korea* were always a treat. If in the middle of reading an article I thought, *Damn, this is good!* I was sure to find 'Editor Hwang Sunwoo' printed at the bottom of the page. It was so cool that she travelled the world interviewing stars like Tilda

Swinton, Alain de Botton, Jeff Koons, Annie Ernaux, Jean-Jacques Sempé, Lee Ufan and Paul Auster.

The first time I met Sunwoo in person was at a flea market. She was with graphic designer Lee Ari. Back then, I would've never imagined we'd all end up living in the same building, with Sunwoo and me sharing a nice apartment that we bought together. Sunwoo and I had similar tastes and would often bump into each other at pubs, concerts or music festivals. For six years, we hung out only on occasion, and though we barely saw each other's faces, we were always chatting online about our cats. Whenever sleep evaded me, I'd go on Twitter to post my random thoughts, and sure enough, I'd always get a reply from Sunwoo, who was also wide awake. Hwang Sunwoo was once the queen of insomnia. And for a long time, I, too, wrestled with sleep.

For years, Sunwoo and I maintained an online friendship, and the more we spoke, the more I realized how much we had in common: Sunwoo was born in May 1977 and I was born in December 1976, but our births were both registered as a month later than our real birthdates. We both have older brothers born in 1975 and who were the better-looking sibling when we were kids. Our brothers also have similar-sounding feminine names – Hayoung and Sunyoung.

Because Sunwoo had enrolled in school early, we were in the same year. We are both from Busan – Sunwoo from Gwanganri, and I from Haeundae – meaning we both grew up by the beach. Not only did we both leave Busan to attend university in Seoul, we also both went to Yonsei University; Sunwoo was an English major, while I was a Korean language major. When we started living together, we uncovered even *more* of these random similarities. We both have overlapping tastes, especially in music and our alcoholic beverages of choice, so naturally we were regulars at a lot of the same cafes and pubs during and after our uni years. There were many occasions when we belatedly learnt that we'd gone to the same concert. I've always thought it would be fun if we could retrace our steps. I have no doubt we had crossed paths many times in university corridors, sat at the table next to each other in the same pub, stood in the same line for the toilets at some festival, sat in the same row during a concert.

Like the ending scene in *Comrades: Almost a Love Story*, perhaps we'd walked past each other in a sea of strangers before our first ever meeting. After discovering all these coincidences, the fact that we had once lived life not knowing each other is both fascinating and a shame.

Six years after we first met, Sunwoo and I finally

hung out one on one. I remember that day clearly. We chatted through a round of wine, then beer and then whisky. Sunwoo was open to whatever topic I brought up, and though she knew a lot, she was never a show-off. But more than our shared interests, we fancied ourselves comedians and shared the same humour, bursting into laughter at random moments. This first meeting was followed by frequent trips to the movies and art exhibitions and late nights chatting over drinks with music playing in the background – we became close. Sunwoo was the most charismatic conversation partner. After we'd spilled our hearts to each other, I learnt that Sunwoo, too, was done with living alone and was searching for a different way of life. The more we got to know each other, the more I found myself wondering, *What if it's her?* I had a place I had my sights on, you see, but I couldn't buy it alone. I needed a partner in crime, and I wanted to live with her.

OTHERS: A FOREIGN COUNTRY

Sunwoo   Whenever I exit an airport in the subtropics, my nose is the first sense to react. I've suffered from sinus infections my whole life, making it really difficult to breathe in dry weathers. And so, there's nothing I love more than landing in a Southeast Asian city or an island like Saipan, stepping out of the airport and walking into the embrace of the heat and humidity. It feels just like hugging a warm puppy. Besides, that first step off a stuffy plane is when I'm greeted by a country's own unique blend of air and sunlight, greenery and scenery, architecture and aromas.

People, too, possess their own climates and cultures, and spending time with someone is like exploring a new destination. The saying 'Hell is dealing with other people' is not entirely untrue, but to me, there's no better fun than interacting with others. Our very own worldview, our music tastes, our interests and the way we speak, our expressions and actions, our beliefs and imaginations, the way we joke . . . every one of these factors colour in our own unique aura and charm. And if we can respect other people's differences as polite travellers, we'll witness many beauties different from ours.

I first met Hana on Twitter. She was nicknamed Tol, or Bean (@kimtolkong). I remember meeting her in person for the first time, when she visited Ari's and my flea market booth. She looked like her username, round-faced like an acorn. The world's a funny place – who would've thought the three of us there that day would later become neighbours, and that Hana and I would live in an apartment that we bought together? Around that time, I learnt that Hana was editor-in-chief at *Catchball Weekly*, which wasn't just a blog, but also a club. I eventually joined. Contrary to what its name suggests, the blog posted only sporadically about club activities. The club essentially consisted of a group of people bonding over the motto, 'Let's idle away the hours, friends!' They'd meet up whenever they had free time and go somewhere with a nice view to play a relaxed game of catchball. Everyone used neon Velcro gloves and cute balls decorated with pictures of Pororo or Doraemon – it was that kind of club.

Aside from running *Catchball Weekly*, Hana also

blogged about her six-month-long travels around South America. It was a place that I'd always dreamt of visiting, but I'd never got around to actually planning a trip. After quitting her job at an advertising agency, Hana poured her free time into writing blog posts that showcased her prowess as a seasoned copywriter. Entranced by her words, I devoured every one of her posts as if she were an idol and I her biggest fangirl.

On her goals and the intention behind starting *Catchball Weekly*, Hana wrote:

A person shouldn't pride themselves
on the number of square feet in their house or the
brand of car they drive, but on their friends.
Not on how accomplished or how powerful their
friends are.
But how well they can cook, how well they can eat,
how soundly they sleep, how well they can sing, how
honest they can be,
how many drinks you've had together,
and how many silly memories – those are the things
you can truly be proud of.

In her group of friends, Hana is always the core – the leader who brings her teammates together. She is sure of her worldview, and instead of keeping it to herself, shares it with her community. But as her cohabitant, I've seen her in her moments of darkness and solitude. As I watch her – an introvert who likes to recharge by reading a book – chase after the value of community, I realize the multiplicity within us. Unlike Hana, I'm practically a transfer station through which human relationships come and go, the textbook example of a social butterfly. But deep down, I'm more comfortable in small groups of no more than three, and am the type to ask a friend to drink with me not because I crave the company, but because I simply love alcohol. As an extrovert who is in some ways closed off and selfish, I'm fascinated by how my sense of self can continue to grow despite this irony. The thought that it'd be nice to live with Hana sprouted easily in my mind, but what made it grow was the hope of holding her positivity close, of always being surrounded by it.

Hana always says, 'Friends are a social and emotional safety net.' True enough, Hana and I have always been there to catch the other. Like a climate zone with its own temperature and humidity, a person can become their cohabitant's entire environment. I say this as the biggest beneficiary of living with a pro at pinpointing and hyping up a person's strengths – Hana aka The Compliment Bombarder (a nickname she got while hosting *Chek It Out: Kim Hana's Flank Attack*, a podcast introducing the latest 'chek's, or 'books'). We drink a lot, and our stash of silly memories is ever-growing. We're good at cooking and we sure know how to eat. I should be proud of these things – my cohabitant taught me that. I've discovered a new continent named Kim Hana; another world opens.

MANGWON HOF
STOLE MY HEART

Hana   Life's sceneries are all different. We could be grouped under a range of categories like 'big family', 'nuclear family', 'house owner' or 'apartment owner', but everyone's homes will look different. A house's layout or concept is not simply an abstract vibe; it can be a specific example of somebody's dream home. My dream home was Mangwon Hof. But before we get into Mangwon Hof, I'd like to introduce my friend Kim Mincheol. She's authored a bunch of cool books like *A Record of Every Day* and *A Day's Tastes*. I blurbed her book *A Trip for Every Day*.

I first met Mincheol in January 2005. It was my first day of work as assistant manager at the TBWA Korea office, and she was introduced to me as my team's new copywriter. Just from her name, I'd assumed she'd be a man. Since there had been no junior copywriter in my previous company, Mincheol became my first direct report. I affectionately nicknamed her Mr Cheol because of her manly sounding name.

For two years we worked on many projects together and became close. The highlights of my portfolio include the campaigns for SK Telecom's *White Book on Modern Living*, Naver's *Every Knowledge in the World*, LG XCanvas, Hyundai Card and the car brand Infinity – and they were all achieved with Mr Cheol as my co-copywriter. A perfect duo, we made up for what the other lacked and relied on each other. Before long, Mr Cheol became one of my most trusted friends. I can recall vividly the day Mincheol went on a blind date with Jung Ilyeong, and then the day she introduced me to him. I called Ilyeong 'The Star that Appears in the Day' – 'Day Star' for short – because of his quiet yet constant presence, and my nickname for the couple was 'Mr Cheol-Day Star'. After quitting my job, Mr Cheol-Day Star and I went from being just colleagues to best and long-time drinking buddies. If there's one thing I regret about my South American trip, it's missing their wedding.

After getting married, Mr Cheol-Day Star rented a place in the Mangwon neighbourhood. As expected of a couple who can hold their liquor, they decorated their home like a pub. I called it 'Mangwon Hof', and it became my personal go-to pub where I was close with the owners. Since Mangwon Hof was on a jeonse lease – a rental system where tenants pay a lump-sum deposit in lieu of rent, typically lasting between one to two years – it saw several location changes until its owners bought a property, and the homey pub finally settled down in an apartment in Mangwon-dong's Hangang Park. With the help of an interior design company, Mr Cheol-Day Star officially transformed their home into a proper, cosy pub. They lived right by Mangwon Reservoir Sports Park, a view which I could enjoy from their apartment.

I wasn't the biggest fan of apartments. I grew up in an apartment, but it was right by Haeundae Beach, and although our apartment was on the ground floor, we could always catch a glimpse of the sea. In the summer, the kids in our apartment complex would dash out of their homes in their swimsuits, a float around their waists, and run straight towards the beach. When I turned nineteen and moved to Seoul, I lived in all sorts of apartments – walk-ups, shoeboxes and rooms in family homes. The longer I spent living alone, the more my collection of one-person furniture confirmed my status as a fully fledged bachelorette. But when at last loneliness washed in, I began to seek out a new living arrangement. The picture I'd drawn of my ideal housing situation began with a big family home. I found apartments in Seoul to be stifling, and thought it'd be nice to have a place with a few rooms and a little courtyard that I could share with friends.

Being a chronic namer of things, I called this vision of mine 'The Unoccupied House Project'. And because I referred to this dream of mine so often by name, my friends would think of me whenever they chanced upon a suitable listing. Why 'unoccupied house', you ask? Well, I'd heard that houses owned by people who were living overseas were often way cheaper than market price. I spoke so much about The Unoccupied House Project to my Frivolous Knowledge Club, an informal seminar where members took turns to share about a particular topic, that fellow member and architect Im Taebyeong once took it upon himself to take us on a little field trip around Yeonhui-dong to look at houses. The houses and gardens were all fancy and huge, but since they weren't 'unoccupied', they cost a fortune. The size and orientation of the rooms, too, were too varied, which could cause conflicts between housemates. After Taebyeong's first tour, we went on a few more trips to look at houses, but that picture in my mind remained a distant, unattainable dream.

But then I fell in love with Mangwon Hof. It had unobstructed views, just like the apartment I grew up in, and didn't feel stuffy at all. Unlike most apartment complexes, it was a single building and wasn't cramped between other buildings. It was also in a good location. Though technically in Mangwon-dong, which at the time was up-and-coming, Mangwon Hof was a considerable distance away from the main area, safe from the bluster of gentrification and commotion. Funnily enough, despite my longing for peace and quiet, I spent a long time living in a majorly gentrified area. Before 'Seochon' even got its name, I lived in the idyllic Hyoja-dong, just west of the Gyeongbokgung Palace. But at some point, the neighbourhood opened up, and soon I was surrounded by construction sites. Having spent ten years there, I was quite sad when I was eventually chased out by the incessant drilling and banging, crowds of strangers, ever-changing streets and skyrocketing rent. Mangwon Hof, however, seemed to be a safe distance away from such dangers. Mr Cheol-Day Star's apartment measured about 99m². It had three rooms, two bathrooms, a spacious living room completed by a veranda, and a small storeroom – perfect for two. Before Sunwoo and I became close, I'd only kept Mangwon Hof in the back of my mind. But once Sunwoo got on my radar, I revived my dream of living in a proper home with a proper housemate.

TWO TYPES OF PEOPLE

Sunwoo 'There are two types of people in this world' – this is both a cliché that I fish out whenever I'm stuck on my first line for an article and a truth that I keep rediscovering as I live with Hana. There are people who stress over having to put on an outfit before going out, and those who can't stand the thought of going out in the same outfit twice. The former finds comfort in wearing the same outfit, while the latter craves the thrill of change. Some people can't have music playing in the background while they work, and some work best switching between at least five different windows on their computer. On vacation, there are people who put their phones away, choosing to remember the destination by taking in the sights and sounds, and those who must always be connected to the internet and rely on their phone to tell them where they are or what to do next.

In all of these instances, the former describes Hana and the latter, me. Hana sees washing up as a sort of meditation, while I think of cooking as playtime. If Hana finds a body soap she fancies, she'll prove her love by purchasing many bottles of the same soap. Meanwhile, I like collecting soaps of different scents from brands I can't even remember so that I can line them up in the shower and have my pick of the day. Just off the top of my head I could list twenty other things where we differ, but filling up a whole page with examples would be just as much of a bore as the cliché that kicked off this essay. Anyway, whenever I look at my cohabitant, I'm reminded that I'm some- one who lives complicatedly, always juggling multiple balls at a time and running around in a frazzled state.

There will be differences that we simply can't under- stand. Through Hana, I learnt that not everyone in the world goes wild over strawberries, but it's a fact that I often forget and hence surprises me every time we go to the supermarket. And as I pop strawberries into my mouth, one after the other, I'm always gripped by a strange feeling tinged in sadness. *How can she not like this?* I wonder. (Hana prefers watermelons, Korean melons and pears.) But just because two people live together, doesn't mean they have to like the same things. Just as two people can understand each other and not be close, two people who don't understand each other can be there for each other and live in harmony. Refraining from throwing looks at someone or judging them just because they're different from you is the first step to mutual respect.

But some differences can lead to conflict. Imagine pairing a minimalist who spends wisely to avoid clutter with a shopaholic for whom shopping is both their greatest happiness and only form of stress relief. Some people make sure to return things to their original place, while some people like giving their things a new home after each use. Of course, there's a huge difference between the time it takes for them to find a particular thing. In these instances, too, Hana is the former and I'm the latter. I'll write more in detail about our biggest difference and the catalyst for most of our disagreements, but for now, let me say this: as the latter and, therefore, the main troublemaker, I am doing my best to change my ways. Our arguments have dulled the corners of our stubbornness, and as we continue to test each other's boundaries, the rigid outline of our differences is starting to bend.

Observing others from a close distance and living with them has taught me several life lessons. I've learnt that the world is replete with propensities and choices that are vastly different from mine, and

I've grown aware of striking parts of my personality and traits that I hadn't noticed before. The greatest lesson, perhaps, is the fact that it is totally possible for two very different people to respect and live with each other. As much as we're different, we're also very similar – one of the many things we share is our love for books. We express this differently, of course. While I'm the type to buy a bunch of books – half of which I'll leave untouched – for the sake of hitting the fifty thousand won minimum spend to receive two thousand won in store credits, Hana, who can't stand the sight of books piling up, only buys one book at a time. Naturally, the books that I order on impulse are always spilling into Hana's precious space. My chaotic mountain of books, however, isn't completely useless. When Hana first started her podcast *Chek It Out*, she would go through the pile of books that I'd received in the mail and chucked in a corner of the living room and pick one out to read. An avid reader and someone who obsesses over things easily, Hana would rave to me about all the good books she'd excavated from my pile. In exchange for keeping up a constant supply of books for Hana to peruse, I get a personal book reviewer who'll tell me which books are worth my time. I don't buy less books, but I do read a lot more.

If similarities bring people together, differences fill

the space between them. Would someone similar to me make a good cohabitant? Perhaps despite understanding them wholly, I'd get sick of them and run away. But by living with Hana – my complete opposite – I've become less greedy, somewhat tidier and a little more relaxed (or so I'd like to think). I hope that Hana, too, sometimes feels relieved that she's living with someone different from her. When she learns about the sweet-and-sour wonder of Jukhyang strawberries, when we polish off a box of fried chicken without having to give up our favourite parts (because I prefer drumsticks and she likes wings), when the space between us fills.

CATCH THAT APARTMENT!

Hana   Once, I'd sneakily convinced Mr Cheol-Day Star to invite Sunwoo and me to their home. Sunwoo and I showed up at Mangwon Hof, wine in hand. As expected of a couple who takes their alcohol seriously, Mr Cheol-Day Star showed us the best service. With great music, fancy anju to nibble on and enthralling conversation topics, they coaxed us into tipsiness, and before we knew it we were plunging straight into drunkenness – the classic drinking narrative! That day, like any other day at Mangwon Hof, we drank and laughed to our hearts' content. The shelves around us were neatly and beautifully arranged with books, CDs, plates made by Mr Cheol and Day Star's impressive figurine collection. Their house was spacious and tidy and it didn't feel cluttered. Since they, too, were bookworms, they'd turned one of their rooms into a library furnished with rows of bookshelves. After whipping up a delicious meal in the kitchen, the couple came out to the living room. Beyond the wide glass window, Mangwon Reservoir Sports Park's outdoor stadium was spread out in its full glory. When night fell, the stadium lights came on, basking the pitch in serenity. Everything was perfect.

Clinking my glass against Sunwoo's, I casually remarked: *Isn't this just so perfect? Can you believe this view? It'd be so nice to live with someone in an apartment like this.* Meanwhile, Sunwoo was getting comfortable in the big home with a gorgeous view; emotions were starting to stir in her, it seemed.

After that day, I told Sunwoo that my dream home was one exactly like Mr Cheol-Day Star's. Sunwoo, too, loved that apartment. And so I proposed the idea of combining our jeonse deposits and taking out a bank loan to buy a house together. Sunwoo, however, was hesitant for a few reasons:

1. The commute from Mangwon-dong to her workplace in Nonhyeon-dong was way too long.
2. The apartment building was far away from the main area and the street it was on felt eerie.
    2-1. Besides, there were no convenience stores around.
3. She'd never thought of actually *buying* a house.

4. Even if we pooled together our jeonse deposits, we wouldn't have enough money.

Looking back, those were perfectly legitimate reasons; but at the time, I was completely confident we could overcome any obstacles. I didn't disregard Sunwoo's concerns, but I believed I could win her over with passion and earnestness. Just to be clear, I'm not the type to chase after material goods. I don't buy things just because there's an irresistible sale, and I don't drool over the latest gadgets and what-not. I buy things only when I really want them and if they're within my budget, and I use my things for a long, long time. I take very good care of my things, and find joy in using them, even when I use them daily. And so this apartment was the exception – I was *obsessed*.

Besides, I was a copywriter.

I knew I could convince Sunwoo, line by line:

1. If the bus takes the Gangbyeon Expressway from Nonhyeon-dong, Mangwon is only two stops away from where you currently live. The house is also close to the expressway.
2. As for the eerie street, you'll be driving home most of the time. If you ever find yourself

walking back home, I'll come get you with a baseball bat. (I wasn't afraid of eerie streets.)

2-1. Since the apartment is far away from the main area, we'll have peace and quiet. If there's something you need, I'll get on my bike and go get it for you. Besides, you can get anything delivered to your doorstep these days, even groceries and laundry.

3. Moving every two years puts us in such a precarious position. Now that we're in our forties, we should look to find a more permanent, stable place to live and start consolidating our scattered expenses and lives.

Now, to conquer point number four. If I were more practical and economical, I would've understood that the last point meant a definite no. Instead, I simply saw it as another hurdle, the last push before we were on our way to buying a house. I hadn't the faintest idea of how much I actually had, and how much I could borrow from the bank.

4. Since we're buying a house, we can take out a secured loan. I heard that'll give us 70 per cent of the whole amount. And then all we have to

do is work hard and slowly pay off the loan. Living together in a proper home, our life will become more stable, and our daily expenses will be reduced.

Without doing any proper research, I worked hard on persuading Sunwoo, and it seemed my confidence was starting to sway her (or perhaps she'd assumed there must be a good reason as to why I wouldn't shut up). At last, an apartment appeared on the market. It was right next to Mr Cheol-Day Star's and on a decently high floor. We went to see it together. I loved it right away. But it was on for a few hundred thousand won more than Mr Cheol-Day Star had paid for their apartment.

Mr Cheol-Day Star had managed to buy theirs for cheap because it had been listed as an urgent sale. In the meantime, however, property prices had skyrocketed. Thinking that we were getting ripped off, we went to enquire at a different realtor, but to our disappointment, every house was in that same price range. Mangwon-dong had become a hotspot, and even the quietest streets were getting swept up in its popularity. Still, I wanted that house desperately. I was anxious we might miss our chance, but since I wasn't buying the house on my own, I couldn't force my cohabitant to make a decision. True enough, in our hesitation, the listing was sold. We'd missed it. It was a big shame. Sunwoo, too, seemed to regret stalling on the decision. We would've remained a bit more hopeful if the apartment complex were comprised of several blocks, but it was a small development, and it seemed unlikely that another apartment would appear on the market any time soon.

With our sights set on Mangwon-dong, we'd go house hunting in the neighbourhood during our free time. I went with Sunwoo mostly, but sometimes, I went with my friend Hwang Yeongju, who was a Mangwon-dong resident. Since the day Mangwon Hof stole my heart, no other house had struck my fancy. But beggars can't be choosers. I started leaning towards an apartment that fell within our budget. It was surrounded by shops and public transport and the walk towards it wasn't eerie. Still, I wasn't completely sold. Just as Sunwoo and I were having many of the same discussions, going back and forth on whether we should sign the contract, we received a call saying that a new listing had just gone on the market – an apartment in the same building as Mangwon Hof! But there was just one problem. One of the biggest reasons I'd fallen so in love with Mangwon Hof was its gorgeous view of the reservoir. While Mr Cheol-Day

Star's apartment faced southeast, the one we were being offered faced southwest and hence didn't have the same view. We were sorely disappointed, but went to check out the place anyway.

A WOMAN OF THE SUN

Hana   In our home, we've got a hefty brass pocket compass. Every time Sunwoo moved into a new place, her father would come all the way from Busan and use the instrument to check which direction Sunwoo's new apartment was facing. Sunwoo's father would carefully read his compass to make sure that his precious daughter was moving into a south-facing home. (My parents, on the other hand, didn't care about where I lived or moved. Whenever I moved into a new place, they'd visit me only if they had a wedding to attend in Seoul.) Thanks to her father, Sunwoo had woken up every morning in her Sangsu-dong apartment feeling like a dried seaweed basking on white sand. Streaming through the linen curtains, the sun would warm her cheeks, and nudge her awake with its dazzling light. The whole thing sounds absolutely cruel to a sensitive sleeper like me, but there's no feeling that Sunwoo loves more than a house doused in sun from morning to noon.

You see, Sunwoo *loves* the sun. She likes exercising out in the sun and going to festivals on the sunniest days. She says it's because the sun's written in her saju, her destiny. Come monsoon season, she grows depressed, and when she has to stay in to rush a deadline, she gets very stressed. Given her sunny disposition, we set out to buy a house that would always be bright.

The day we were informed of the apartment mentioned in the previous chapter, Sunwoo was caught up with work, so I went with Yeongju to look at it. The open front door might have something to do with it, but my goodness, the entire living room was flushed in the brightest orange glow. It was autumn, and since the apartment was southwest-facing, the setting sun stretched all the way in. The elderly couple who lived there had a lot of things, and all the mouldings and doorframes were coated in cherry-coloured vinyl, so the apartment wasn't exactly pretty, but the layout was neat and the house was clean. Instead of a reservoir, there was a view of the sky and the Han River. Blocked by criss-crossing expressways, the river looked more like a slender hairtail fish; only its glistening radiance proved its existence. But I was most captivated by the bright orange flush. I knew immediately that the woman of the sun, Sunwoo, would love it too.

The problem, again, was that the apartment was way more expensive than the house we'd been considering. Sixty million won more expensive, to be exact. But I didn't want to let go of yet another house. It was back to persuading Sunwoo. *Sure, it's beyond our means, and sure, it's way out of our budget. But the amount we'd be forking out is as great as the house we'll live in!* Welcome to the thought process of someone with zero economic sense. But Sunwoo herself was starting to think of that sixty million won as the price to pay for missing out on that first house. After many attempts at winning Sunwoo over – *A river view is so much better than a reservoir view! The house will always be flooded with light!* – we went to see the house together. But the minute we stepped into the house, I broke out in a cold sweat.

It was eleven in the morning, the darkest hour in a southwest-facing house. Once the door swung open, I freaked out on the inside: *I'm so screwed!* Even as noon approached, the house remained dark, and we had to switch on the ceiling lights. I realized then why a house should be viewed more than once. As sweat rolled down my forehead, I couldn't tell from Sunwoo's expression what was running through her mind. I let out a silent scream when I opened the bedroom door, and another one when I switched on the kitchen lights. Once she'd gotten a good look at the entire house, Sunwoo gazed out the window. She saw the hairtail-shaped river in the distance and the green crowns of plane trees. 'Thanks for showing us around,' we said before heading to the lift. I was too flustered to say or do anything. Just as I'd expected, the first thing Sunwoo said was, 'This house is dark in the mornings, huh?' I assured her that come afternoon, the house would be bathed in a much warmer hue of light that would stay for way longer than in any southeast-facing house. But my voice lacked strength. I knew just how much Sunwoo loved having light in the morning, and how much she loved the vibe of a perfectly south-facing house. At last, Sunwoo said, 'The plane trees outside looked just like waves.'

And then in the car, she said, 'I liked it.'

In that moment, I heard all the plane trees in the world rustle.

I EVEN THOUGHT
ABOUT MARRIAGE

Sunwoo   There's a line in an old song that goes, 'I even thought of marrying you.' It's a song about a man crying over a woman whom he loved a lot, and to whom he is saying his final good-bye. Is marriage a relationship's final destination or pinnacle of success? I certainly don't think so now, but there was a time when I'd thought about getting married. Not because there was someone whom I deeply loved, but just because the thought would flit across my mind now and then. When I was in my twenties, I'd always pictured marriage in my future. Media portrayals of the ideal women in their mid- to late thirties had a big influence on me. Teachers, presidents, diplomats ... As a little girl, my ambitions revolved around the limited occupations that I knew and, up until my twenties, my imagination remained rather dull; I grew up assuming I'd one day become the universal version of a woman. When I was younger, dating was never an issue. As an adult, I was always seeing someone, and so naturally I thought I'd marry one of my boyfriends once I reached a certain age. But later, I realized my consideration of marriage had nothing to do with the depth of my relationships or the degree of my love; rather, it was the result of socio-cultural influence. The first time I went on a blind date, I wondered what it'd be like if I married the guy, and later on, after seeing someone for three months, I imagined marrying him. But no matter how many times I toyed with the idea of marriage, for decades, it never became a reality.

I think there are many women who are like me in my twenties – that is, the me who believed that I would get married the way I'll eat when I'm hungry, or land a job after I graduate – someone who has yet to ask themselves if their personality or temperament suits a married lifestyle, and if the way they want to live life can be squeezed into the box labelled 'family'. I've seen so many married men who dread the week-ends they have to spend with family and whine about how this isn't the sort of life they want. What I always fail to say straight to their faces is that they aren't the ones bearing the brunt of marriage, household labour, child rearing – it's their wives.

There are times when I think, *I'm so glad I'm not married.* I see how my married colleagues struggle to balance work and raising their children, and I'm not confident that I can live in full concentration mode, always dividing up my time so strictly. I'm even less confident when I look at their husbands, who always seem to be so relaxed whether it's in the office or their personal lives. I'm relieved I don't have to live as someone's daughter-in-law. In South Korea, going from the princess of the family, a competent worker or a care-free individual to a daughter-in-law is a significant drop in rank. I've never heard about a *son*-in-law who gets nagged because he doesn't call home enough, who busies in the kitchen for hours during the holidays or who is told to make sure their daughter has this and that. What's scary to me is that the tendency to get excited about fulfilling the role of the good daughter-in-law is somehow inherent. That desire is reflected in Soo Shin-ji's manga masterpiece, *No, Thank You* (*Myeoncuragi*), which depicts that period of time when a woman voluntarily does her best because she wants to please her in-laws and be loved by them.

Hana's parents often invite me to eat with them. They tell me they used to worry about their daughter living alone, but feel assured now that I'm by her side. When I'm at the table, I do my part – responding to her mother's small talk and clinking glasses with her father who loves to drink. It's nice to look at them and see parts of Hana that I appreciate, and I'm so thankful that they've passed all their best traits on to her. I return home, belly full of the meat they'd lovingly grilled for me, and after some time, I'll wonder how they're doing and ask after them. There's no need for me to go over to Hana's parents house to peel fruits or do the washing-up, and there's no pressure to prove my filial piety. If I – the appointed chef – have to work late or go on a business trip, my mum, who believes that there's nothing more important than eating properly, is the first person to worry about Hana. 'What's Hana going to do about her meals?' she'd ask. If daughters-in-law were not bogged down by familial obligations, but thanked by their in-laws for being by their child's side, how much lighter and happier would they feel?

MOOCHING OFF A WUSS

Hana Since the apartment we wanted far exceeded our budget, we had to take some serious measures. Sunwoo and I endeavoured to gather funds from wherever we could. After asking our parents to think of it as if we were getting married, we borrowed from them and looked into mortgage loans. And despite the minus sign in her account, Mr Cheol said she could lend us some money, an offer we didn't take but for which we will always be grateful. After a trip to the bank one day, Sunwoo returned with news that we could take out a bigger loan than we thought. Since the loan could be borrowed only under one person, Sunwoo decided to take one for the team. When discussing the monthly loan payment, we opted for the minimum because although Sunwoo received a monthly salary working as a department head in a big company, I was a freelancer with an unpredictable monthly income. To make up for the fact, I promised to repay a chunk of the loan whenever I received a big payment. After punching in the calculations, we concluded that if we scraped together every cent from our salaries, we'd be able to pay off the mortgage eventually.

And so we said, 'Looks like we're signing the contract.'

And we did. It wasn't our first time going to a realtor's office, but sitting down to sign a contract to *buy* a home felt very different. After carefully reading through the contract, we paid the deposit, wrote our names side by side and stamped on our seals. There, all done! We had a house under our names. Freed at last from nerves, we walked out of the realtor's office and breathed in the fresh air. The weather that day was clear. All smiles, I turned to my official cohabitant and partner in crime and proudly proclaimed, 'We bought a house!'

I raised my hand to give Sunwoo a high five but stopped short. A shadow was drawn across her face.

'What's wrong?'

'We're under a mountain of debt now . . .'

Hearing the dread in Sunwoo's voice, I burst into laughter. *We just bought a house and she's acting like it's a punishment!* I found it both incredulous and adorable. At the same time, my trust in her crystallized – at least now I could be perfectly certain that we'd written down the correct names in the contract, and that Sunwoo wasn't planning on running away with the money. That my cohabitant was someone who was economically responsible.

'Aigo, you big wuss! We're going to be fine! This is supposed to be a happy day!'

Sunwoo forced a smile. I still laugh when I think about that day.

But me, I don't know if Sunwoo considers me as someone she can trust. I only learnt about this recently, but a bank won't simply loan you however much money you need. The limit depends on the borrower's credibility. The bank will first assess how stable your income is, and how capable you are of paying back the loan. Even though as a freelancer I was earning more than at my office job, I didn't have a steady income and my credit card application had been rejected once – according to the bank's standards, I wasn't a borrower who could be trusted. In South Korea, it's practically impossible for a single freelancer to buy a house. (Unfair, I know!) And so I realized: we were only able to buy a house because Sunwoo had held an office job for eighteen years. Because although I'd been the daring one, pestering her to buy a house with me, there was very little that I could've contributed.

And it was out of ignorance that I'd had the audacity to keep bugging Sunwoo about buying a house. Had I understood the world of credits and loans and my limitations, I wouldn't have acted that way. It's true what they say: the bravest people are fools.

After realizing all this, I said to Sunwoo, 'I basically mooched off you ... I clung on to a fastidious office worker, got her to buy a house and now I'm driving her convertible.'

I'd sold my car because parking in Seochon was a big headache, but I love driving. When Sunwoo left her company at Nonhyeon-dong to start a new job located in Hapjeong, which is much closer and more convenient by the maeul bus, I got to take her car whenever I had to go to work or get groceries. Thanks to Sunwoo, I live in a nice apartment and drive a fancy car. Hehe. Anyway, the wuss and the moocher are slowly paying off their debt and living very happily together.

LET'S BECOME SKILLED DEBTORS

Sunwoo   My first order of business after quitting my job was to binge-watch *Game of Thrones*. Eight seasons long and highly addictive, the show wasn't the type to let its viewers go after just one episode so they could catch a good night's sleep before work the next day. Now that I had a long break before starting my new job, I bid my cohabitant goodbye and headed straight for Westeros. Among the houses fighting over the Iron Throne is one represented by a golden lion – House Lannister, a family with an unquenchable greed for power. In every episode, one of the Lannisters would recite their family motto, 'A Lannister always pays his debts.' Here, debt usually takes the shape of revenge or fair compensation. Keeping a meticulous record of everything they owed and were owed, the Lannisters slowly made their way up to control of the throne.

If my family had a motto of our own, it would be,

'Never rent. It's a waste of money.' My dad held a government job until he retired, and the rest of my family members were mostly educators or office workers, so it was only natural that we felt strongly about saving our meagre salaries. The good thing about being raised by people who always played it safe is that I learnt to walk with my eyes trained on the ground. Not even seductive promises of riches can make me look up and step into a hole. In fact, you're more likely to win the lottery than hear of a Hwang who'd fallen for a pyramid scheme or a vacant land scam. On the flipside, we don't know a thing about investing or taking high risks that could bring high reward. Growing up in a family where no one ever went broke nor made it big, debt, to me, was an unwelcomed burden – something to be ashamed of and to get rid of quickly.

Right. I was a wuss. When I went to uni and met a friend whose family ran their own business, I realized just how differently we were raised. Instead of helping out with the family business during the breaks, my friend would drive the family car around town, and instead of splitting the bill, she would offer to pay for everyone at the table and, in turn, never felt bad when someone else offered to foot the bill. But it wasn't only because she was rich or liked to throw money around. Rather, she knew how to make big transactions and had faith in the liquidity of her capital. In fact, her family would often say this: 'Going into debt is a skill.'

The day we walked out of the realtor's office after stamping our seals and paying the contract fee, Hana was shocked to see the expression on my face and asked if I was feeling ill. As I stumbled forwards, numb from the knees down, I, too, could feel that I'd gone pale. And of course I had! For the first time in my life, I was hundreds of millions of won in debt. The mortgage loan we received from the bank was only 20 per cent of the purchase price, and though in my name, it was split equally between Hana and me, but once the minus sign flashed into my mind, I was filled with dread. While I was proud of myself for buying my first home, I knew I was tying myself to a hefty burden. Hana had turned to me and teased, 'Aigo, you big wuss!'

Fast-forward to two years after that fateful day, what's happened to that big wuss? Imagine if a person who hates snakes were forced to live with a snake. She'd probably do her best to avoid getting bitten, and maybe even learn a few things about taming the snake. To give you the short summary, we paid off half of our loan in a year. We've been saving every cent so that we can be released from debt as soon as possible. Since buying a house – the biggest purchase

I've ever made – I've wanted for nothing else. My best drinking pal lives in the same house as me *and* I have a kitchen that I can use however I like. There's no reason for me to go out to a pub; we can have all the fun we want in our apartment. And compared to the joy I feel from shopping my stress away, going on vacation or buying pretty yet useless things, the satisfaction of saving up a good amount and paying off our loan is much greater. Since our mortgage deal is for ten years, ending it early means that we'll have to pay an early repayment charge. But that doesn't scare me – spent solely focused on paying off our loan, the past year has changed me for good. Funnily enough, debt has been the best motivation to take my financial sense to the next level. I've acquired a new mindset: so what if I'm in a bit of debt? Now, instead of using any extra income like work bonuses to pay off my loan, I put them into investments. I've figured that since the interest rate on our mortgage isn't very high, there's no need to scramble to pay it off, and that it's OK to take things slow. My mum, however, is still as worried as ever. When I ring her on the weekends, she'll ask about the weather, my health and then my debt.

Taking out a huge loan and paying it back has toughened me up. Here's another lesson I've learnt: just because you can't avoid your fear, doesn't mean you have to tackle it straight on. Now that I've taken a step out of the safety zone where I'd spent my entire life, I realize there's no greater danger than the one I'd made up in my mind. Who knows? Maybe the more cowardly a person is, the more they can trust their instincts to protect them from danger.

And so the slightly braver wuss learns something from the Lannisters:

Debt need not be avoided, just paid off properly.

I WAS RAISED BY DEBT

Hana   It is important for cohabitants to have good financial sense. They should know how one another spends, how they think about money and whether or not they're responsible and capable enough to take care of their own finances. Even if cohabitants keep their finances separate, it can be stressful to have a spendthrift and a penny-pincher living under the same roof. Around the time I was debating on whether I should live with Sunwoo, I came across a *New York Times* article titled '13 Questions to Ask Before Marriage'. One of the questions was: what's the most you would spend on a car, a sofa and a pair of shoes? The next time Sunwoo and I met, I asked her the question. I don't remember her answers, but they were all similar to mine. She probably quoted a higher number for the shoe question, though. That day, we asked other questions, too: what's the most you'd spend on a performance, a meal, a bottle of wine, etc.? All our answers were almost the same. Whenever we hung out, I noticed we would spend similar amounts on treating each other to a meal, drink or movie. Our spending habits have never stressed the other out.

Because both of us are tied to the same debt, our financial capability and stability aren't simply our own business. What would happen if, in the middle of repaying our debt, one person became financially incapable or started behaving irresponsibly? In fact, after signing our housing contract, I was hit by a major career crisis. After facing a myriad of challenges, the two-women branding company I'd started with a friend as a side hustle was forced to shut up shop. We'd loved and defended the company for years, and had been trying to break into the field of branding. The sudden loss of our company threw my whole career into ambiguity. I went from being a co-owner to someone who couldn't answer the question, 'So, what do you do for work?'

My mind was fraught with chaos and confusion, but there was no time to think – I had a loan to pay off. Besides, as the person who'd dragged Sunwoo into debt, I didn't want her to see me struggle with my finances or job situation. It was decided then: I'll take on any job that comes. Since I'd had to focus on my company, I often had to pass up lectures and writing commissions. Now, I didn't have the luxury of saying no. Starting all my emails with 'Thank you for the wonderful proposal!' I'd say yes to any opportunities to lecture or write. I would stand for two or three hours addressing students, parents of students, office workers, homemakers, government workers and educators. The reactions I received were as diverse as my audience, and I would travel far and wide to meet them. Every day was hectic. On days when a lecture didn't go well, I would sit in the metro with my head in my hands, promising I'd do better tomorrow.

Looking back, those days were an intense bootcamp. When I first started giving lectures, I would hesitate, forget my lines and sink into the floor whenever I spotted someone's frowning face in the audience. But once I got the hang of it, I could speak in front of any audience, no matter how big. I stopped getting nervous, spoke with ease – and learnt a thing or two about keeping an audience engaged.

I also took on writing commissions of any topic. The pieces that I wrote were later collated and became my book, *The Art of Relaxing*. Sunwoo blurbed it for me. It became a bestseller and the royalties I earned went straight into paying off our debt. My tough training not only resulted in the publication of *The Art of Relaxing* but also an influx of opportunities to do lectures and book talks. Serendipitously, someone who'd attended one of my talks recommended me as a speaker on the YouTube channel *Fifteen Minutes to Change the World* (or *Sebasi Talk*). I was then invited to chat on the podcast *The Daily Life Research Lab* (or *Ilgiso*), which eventually led to my big break, hosting Yes24's *Chek It Out: Kim Hana's Flank Attack*. I kicked off 2018 by speaking on one of the nation's biggest radio stations, MBC. For a week, I guest-hosted their show *Wait a Minute*, and in the following month, I was made the permanent host for their hour-long segment *The Morning that Opens the World*. After that, I spoke more on radio shows, moderated movie screenings and even hosted Naver's *Book Culture Live Broadcast*. Later that July, I became the host of MBC Radio's *On a Starry Night*.

'Shut up and work' – this motto that was born out of debt and unemployment has taken me to so many unexpected places. Perhaps this house has been my biggest lucky charm.

Now, I am a person working three jobs. I'm a brand writer, a stay-at-home essayist and a public speaker. My friends call me the Haemin Sunim of Mangwon-dong. Just as the Buddhist teacher and author didn't stop after publishing his book, *The Things You Can*

See Only When You Slow Down, but instead dived into an even more diverse range of work, I've been living life as a busy bee. (I recently illustrated a whole book called *15 Degrees,* and now I'm writing this book!) I still work on brand projects, and someday, I'd like to give starting my own little company another go. But more than anything, I want to become the most dependable and financially stable cohabitant that I can be. That has become one of my greatest motivations. After one year of living together, Sunwoo and I combined forces and paid off half of our debt. It was debt that whipped me into shape.

KIM HANA, INTERIOR DESIGNER-IN-CHARGE

Hana   A week before Sunwoo could move, I had to move out of my apartment. I left my cats in my friend Ari's care and found a place to store my things until moving day, when Sunwoo and I would move everything into our new apartment together. That week, I stayed with Sunwoo and saw to the interior design of our new apartment. I didn't handle everything myself, of course, I simply assumed the role of the messenger. Shin Haesu from Texture on Texture was our head designer. She'd graduated from Korea University of Arts as an architecture major, and I'd met her at the Seochon pub she was running called pubb. She'd worked on a few interior design projects but after realizing that the work didn't suit her, she decided to call it quits. Thankfully, the last project she took on was the renovation of our home. Sunwoo and I were bringing along our entire life possessions, had a low budget and gave a ridiculously short timeframe, but Haesu and her assistant, department head Jeon Jaehyung, pulled through and brought our vision to life. To this day, I'm grateful for their help. Did I mention it was freezing that December?

Sunwoo had no interest in the whole interior designing process, but since she liked the feel of my old apartment, she left everything up to me. I took it upon myself to come up with one great principle:

As bright as possible!

I'd thought about it with Sunwoo, the woman of the sun, in mind. Since I was the one who'd convinced her to buy the house with me, I wanted to do everything I could to make sure she didn't regret her decision. The first time we viewed the apartment together, it'd looked particularly dark because it was crowded with furniture and things. The mouldings and doorframes were all cherry red, and the kitchen sink area, blocked by a huge refrigerator, was so dark that you couldn't even see the plates without switching on the lights. Since the kitchen was going to be the centre of our home – given it was where Sunwoo, as the main chef, would be the most active – it needed to be spacious. Guided by the principle of brightness, I decided on the following:

1. Let in as much light as possible!
2. Doorframes, mouldings and wallpapers should be light-coloured. If possible, remove all wall mouldings.
3. Redo the sink and move the fridge so that light can enter. Remove all the cabinets on one side of the kitchen to make the area look brighter. Make the sink area white.

I enjoyed the renovation process. Watching my opinions materialize into real spaces felt like I was in a large-scale arts and crafts class. I suppose it was only fun for me because I didn't have to do any of the work. Since I had a clear picture of the house I wanted and my tastes were apparent, Haesu curated lists of materials and textures, and all I had to do was sit back and choose. Besides, our low budget meant a smaller range of options and even giving up on certain things entirely. Among the more crucial decisions was the issue of the bathtub. Nowadays, it's common to get rid of the tub and install a shower booth, but when Sunwoo and I were living alone, the one thing we longed for was a bathtub. In fact, when we first began discussing the possibility of us living together, we'd rushed to buy a bath tray that could hold a glass of wine, a candle and a book. So instead of getting rid of the bathtub, we installed a new one.

Sunwoo and I went shopping for furniture together. Making decisions was fairly easy since we'd already decided on a wooden interior for the living room, and a monochrome colour palette for the study. We picked out black-and-white bookshelves to furnish the walls of our study and bought some modular furniture to create our walk-in closet room. The table, however, required extra consideration; it was going to be the centrepiece of the living room, and the object that would determine a guest's first impression of our home. We were planning on putting a big and beautiful bookcase handcrafted by my best friend Hwang Yeongju in our living room (more on this precious piece of furniture later), and it wasn't easy finding a table that had the perfect weight, texture and colour to complement the bookcase's harmonious hues of walnut and oak. Even if we were to commission a table from a carpenter, how were we going to find matching chairs? If we wanted chairs that were comfortable, built to last *and* aesthetically pleasing, we'd have to risk going broke.

One day, we went to Muji to look for some home goods. Tired from all the shopping, I plopped down on one of the dining sets to rest my feet. And as I always do, I indulged myself in a bit of improv. 'Looks like we're having lobster pasta for dinner!' I sang. Taking my cue, Sunwoo, too, sat down across from me and played pretend. Shorter than most dining sets, the table and chairs were the perfect height for Sunwoo and me, who are quite small ourselves. In fact, it was the most comfortable dining set we'd tried so far. There was just one thing – it wasn't pretty. The table's light oak plywood was put together with coarse black nails and its roundish legs made it look like a student's desk. Meanwhile the chairs were made of bent plywood and were too roundish in shape. 'The height's perfect but it's just so ugly,' we concluded.

Lying in bed that night, I couldn't stop thinking about that dining set and how comfortable it was. When morning came and still the feeling lingered, I spoke to Sunwoo. It was a big no from her. But whenever we went to Muji to pick up something, I'd take another look at the table. I felt strangely attached to it. I even sent photos of it to two friends whose tastes I trusted, but they shared Sunwoo's response. *If only they knew how comfortable it is!* I sulked. But the more I brought it up with Sunwoo, the more she started to think about it, until one day, she gave me the green light. The moment we welcomed the Muji table into our living room, we decorated it with the Danish lamp that had made us squeal when we first saw it. A year has flown by, and that Muji dining table is where we spend most of our time. We write, eat, drink and read on it. Our cats, too, love the chairs. No matter how many times we go over the seats with a tape roller, they're always covered in fur. Even the friends who'd initially said no admitted that the dining set was a good buy once they came over and sat at the table for themselves. It complements the hardwood furniture in the living room, and adds just the right touch of visual weight to the room.

On our one year anniversary of moving in together, Sunwoo and I invited the Texture on Texture team over for dinner. We wanted to thank them for being so accommodating of our tight budget and deadline, and for building us such a pretty house to live in. Our apartment is a well-curated blend of Haesu's and Jaehyung's tastes, their thoughtful consideration and their ideas. Unfortunately for everyone else, the team is no longer taking on interior design projects. Sunwoo and I were the last, lucky ones.

I KNOW BECAUSE I HAVEN'T
GOT MARRIED MYSELF

Sunwoo   The good thing about being unmarried at this age is that I know a secret the world doesn't: it's not the end of the world if you don't get married. I know this because I haven't got married myself. It's true, everything's perfectly fine. When I think about the consequences – both major and minor – of staying unmarried, all I can come up with is that the chances of me getting married will steadily decrease. Of course, I worry about my future every day. *Until what age will I have to continue working now that people are living to be one hundred? What can I do to level up in my career? If I can only access the pension that I've diligently paid into for twenty years when I'm sixty-five, how will I survive if I retire before then? What if the national pension goes bankrupt and all my money is gone? And what if I fall sick and die early? Or if I live a life too long, plagued by minor illnesses? Is it time to sign up for another insurance plan?*

My worries grow by the day. But suppose I was married – would these problems magically disappear? When I talk to my married friends, I learn that rather than facing different problems, the nature of our concerns are actually quite similar. The only difference is perhaps that they have a few more on their list. Child rearing, educating their kids and providing for their parents and in-laws, for instance. These issues are in fact greater, as they must be shared and discussed with their spouses.

Although I think nothing of it now, I wasn't always comfortable with the thought of ageing year after year as an unmarried woman. My mid- to late thirties was a period of anxiety, which stemmed less from my personal circumstances and internal state, and more from the people around me. Even when women who are 'past their prime' are content with their lives, it seems there are people who like throwing pebbles into a perfectly still lake. Once I entered my thirties, I was suddenly swarmed by people who'd gotten their PhDs in busybodying. From sources I was meeting for the first time to neighbourhood strangers and friends whom I hadn't seen in ages, people asked me about my plans for marriage as casually as they would talk about the weather or political relations between the North and South. To my answer, 'No plans yet,' there was a range of responses. First were the sleuths who were genuinely curious as to why. Then the well-wishers who'd mutter, 'Well, things can only look up from here,' as if I was dealing with a severe loss. And lastly, the cruel ones who'd say, 'I guess even people like you have it rough.' Though these words can easily be mistaken for advice or concern, they're actually inconsiderate and rude. If being unmarried was truly a problem, then the unmarried person would be the most concerned about it. Besides, a person's relationship status isn't something you can change simply by pointing it out. But above all, what gives people the right to pry into someone's life as if they're in charge of it? Perceived to be young and naive, unwed women are often subjected to such invasive surveillance.

The good news is, as you approach the end of your 'prime', the busybodies start leaving you alone. Here's what I've learnt: all you need is to maintain mental fortitude or impenetrable nonchalance for a few years. At some point, I made my peace with it. Before, a part of me wanted to defend myself – *It's not because I'm not popular with the guys and can't date anyone!* – but I don't feel the need to any more. So what if I'm unpopular? What's it to you if I've got a potential fiancé or not? I no longer care about appearing desirable; existing for the sake of appealing to a man does nothing for my self-worth or happiness.

At a dinner gathering once, a married man in his forties told us about the 'Gem Theory'. His point was that all the decent women in the world were already taken. 'The real gems are always excavated no matter how deep in the desert they were hidden. Merchants will find a way and pay any price to get a hold of them.' He demonstrated no regard whatsoever for these women's humanity, treating them like exploitable goods with neither agency nor interests. For some reason I always miss the right timing to argue against crude theories like this, and it's only when I get home that everything I could've said would flood into my mind. *Are women goods you can trade? Pretty sure we're capable of making our own choices. And where's the woman's perspective in all of this?* Instead of saying anything out loud, I'd probably only managed a frown. The regret of not speaking out gnawed at me for a long time. Who knows just how many unmarried women's ears and brains had fallen victim to the same nonsense since then? A while later, during an interview that I did for a magazine, I heard about the 'Ms Calculating Theory'. The philosopher I interviewed said that single women in their thirties were becoming more competitive, selfishly chasing credentials instead of love. He told me to lower my standards. Please – as if he knew a thing about the people I'd dated and my relationships.

Besides these two men, there have been many others (coincidentally, all older men) who've made sarcastic remarks about how I'd failed to make the cut or mocked me for having high standards. Even if that were true, I'm always surprised at their audacity to point it out in front of others, but what's *more* surprising is the fact that these rude men have all managed to get married.

As time passed, I understood more clearly: I wasn't anxious because I was unmarried, but because of the people who continually fuelled the flames of my fears and anxieties. *There must be something wrong with you. Who knows what will become of you in the future?* Try as they may, those nosy folk no longer get me down. I know that I'm not a flawed good, just as I am neither full of myself nor impossible to please. I'm just a woman who's gone through some relationships that didn't work out. There have been times when I was too busy or having too much fun to meet someone new, and times when, desperate to be married, I went on date after date, but had no luck finding someone who shared my personal philosophies and lifestyle.

After all is said and done, I remain unmarried, and I'm doing just fine. I contain diverse stories and a complex history known only to me, and cannot be reduced to a careless summary from someone else's lips. Oh, and sorry to disappoint the busybodies, but I am quite happy at the moment.

So, to all my ladies past their prime, if you ever catch yourself thinking, *Is there something wrong with me?* or, *Is it a problem if I don't see a problem?* ask yourself this: is my heart wavering despite the stillness around me? Or is there someone around me throwing rocks in my lake? If that person is just a passing visitor in your life, it wouldn't hurt to ignore them. But if they're close to you, rather than keeping your frustrations bottled up, perhaps it's worth sitting them down for a serious chat about respecting your choices. Our self-worth is more important than maintaining peace in our social circles, and our relationship with ourselves is far more important than our relationships with others. Besides, married folk (rude married folk, in particular) are living proof that being unmarried doesn't mean you're lacking in any way.

WHEN DOES 'I LIVE ALONE' BECOME 'I'M SINGLE'?

Hana   While they're both used to describe single life, the phrases 'I live alone' and 'I'm single' have very different nuances. I suppose the difference depends on the individual, but to me at least, *living alone* feels like a temporary, transitional period before getting married or accepting one's single status, whereas *living as a single* feels like semi-permanence, order, self-restraint and freedom.

When does someone who lives alone become a fully fledged singleton? To answer this question, consider the dilemma of towels. Every home has their own collection of towels with different logos and in different colours. Towels are not marked by an expiration date, and you can keep using them until they fray or are full of holes. Towels that have been laundered too many times will thin, stiffen and lose their absorbancy, but someone who uses them every day won't notice a difference. They'll continue to use their frayed towels, and collect more random towels, until their cabinet is stuffed and messy.

I don't know when I started doing this, but once every two years on 1 January, I'll replace all my towels. Ten face towels, two bath towels, all white. I'll have everything ready before the year ends, and come the first day of the New Year, I'll replace my sponges, loofa, toothbrush, soaps, kitchen linens – everything. The old things will be repurposed as cleaning supplies or thrown out. It's surprisingly inexpensive to buy twelve towels (I suppose that's why towels make great promotional gifts), and contrary to their low cost, having twelve towels that are of the same colour and of equal softness can have a significant impact. Every time I use a soft, clean towel, it feels like I'm taking care of myself, and every time I open my towel cabinet, I see visual proof that my life is in order. Do towels have an expiration date? My answer is yes. The very moment you get new ones.

The gap between living alone and being single is similar to the towel dilemma. How long do you 'live alone' before you become 'single'? There's no fixed duration; it happens simply when you decide to declare yourself single. Until then, that transitional period is like having a stash of miscellaneous towels – the collection somehow started and will only continue to grow. The way I see it, the biggest difference between living alone and being single is whether you view your current life conditions as temporary or semi-permanent.

I know the exact moment I became a single. It was the day I got that beautiful bookshelf I mentioned earlier.

It was an exhibition piece built by my dearest friend and carpenter Hwang Yeongju (I wrote about our on-off friendship in my book, *The Art of Relaxing*). Crafted entirely out of North American hardwood and varnished with eco-friendly oil, the grand and luxurious bookshelf cost me a fortune. How did it come to be in my possession, you ask? Well, one evening, knocking back bokbunja wine, Yeongju had lamented:

'I should be getting ready for my exhibition but I don't even have the money to buy materials.'

'Really? *hiccough* Then ... how about you build me a bookshelf? Something big enough to fill a wall, and that I can pass on to my children. I'll pay!'

In my half-conscious state, I'd signed up to be a sponsor. As luck would have it, a few outstanding freelance payments had been deposited into my account all at once, and I was able to pay Yeongju in full the next day. For a while, Yeongju called me Medici (after the renowned Italian family who were active patrons of the arts). Considering the amount of hard work and time that went into its creation, the bookshelf must've been worth a brand-new car, but since I was only charged for the materials, I got it at the price of a secondhand car.

The massive beauty occupied a whole wall from top to bottom. You wouldn't believe that it was built by a woman who was barely five foot one. It was more than just a piece of furniture to store books; I'd welcomed into my home a massive wave of change. The gorgeous colours and pattern of the walnut and oak, the thick and neat lines, the smooth and warm textures, the rhythm and balance established by each individual shelf – these elements changed the way I saw my house. I was becoming a real adult. I started to think twice before buying anything and only bought things that would match the shelf. My belongings were no longer shoddy, temporary objects waiting to be replaced at some point in the future. Back when I was living alone, the day when I'd replace my belongings with 'proper things' had only existed as a vague concept in my mind. But in my drunken state, I'd let one 'proper thing' into my home, and it had instantly brought order into my life. Call that the power of a beautiful, well-made object. The day this bookshelf came into my life was the day I started living as a single.

I've since bid goodbye to living alone and become someone's cohabitant. The modular bookshelf stands in our living room; we've divided it in half and placed the two halves horizontally on both sides of the living room. Whenever I post a picture of our place on Instagram, I always get comments asking where we got our bookshelf. With a mixture of pride and regret, I say, 'My friend made it for me. It's one-of-a-kind.' Because Yeongju no longer makes furniture. Living in this country has made it difficult for her to continue her work. A furniture company stole this bookshelf design of hers, you see. When Yeongju found out about the plagiarism, she filed a complaint, but given the current laws, little could be done. Ripped off and mass-produced, those copycat bookshelves will never emanate the same charisma as mine. (That darn company will pay for this!!) After a trying decade of carpentry, Yeongju now runs a pub in our neighbourhood (though our country is also tough on business owners). Her pub, Barcelona, is where we celebrated the publication of this book.

I CAN'T GET RID OF ANYTHING

Sunwoo   'Is your daughter an actor?'

When I returned from my business trip, which unfortunately overlapped with our move-in day, Mum told me that the old ajussi from the moving company had asked her this. Apparently, the ajussi had asked if I was an actor after seeing all my clothes. Mum was ecstatic that a complete stranger had proven her case. 'You see why I keep telling you to clear out your wardrobe? Make sure you tidy up in your new house,' she nagged. But there was a flaw in the ajussi's logic: I didn't just have a lot of clothes. I *also* had a lot of books, CDs, vinyl records, cups and plates. When I used to move apartments every two years, I would always tell the moving company that I was a newly-wed. If not they'd send a van too small to transport all of my things.

If having a lot of clothes makes someone an actor, what does that make someone with lots of books,

CDs, vinyl records, cups and plates? Someone on the movers' blacklist, that's for sure. I am a collector. I'm like a crow who likes filling her nest with shiny things. The problem is, those shiny things include miscellaneous crap like silver spoons, cooking foil and stainless-steel lunchboxes.

One day, Hana said to me excitedly, 'Did you know there's a book called *Someone Who Can't Get Rid of Anything*? The title describes you perfectly, so I went ahead and bought it. Make sure you read it.' I didn't say a word. The truth was, I'd bought the book myself and read it because, as my cohabitant had correctly pointed out, the title was so me. I'd also bought *The Life-changing Magic of Tidying*. But just when I was inspired to tidy up, I couldn't find the book anywhere amid the dizzying mess, and alas, I failed to make my life shine. I had too many things and just as many books on having too many things. The first time Hana came over to hang out, she was shocked to see that my walls were totally covered with things. Since then, Hana would come over occasionally when I wasn't home to help me tidy up. I'd seen someone like her before. When I was little, I used to visit my grandmother's house in the countryside. My aunt, who was married and lived near by, would come over and clean my grandmother's house. Like my aunt who liked things to be clean and tidy, I suppose Hana had cleaned my apartment partly because she genuinely wanted to help, and partly because she couldn't stand the sight of the mess.

If I could be allowed an excuse, my previous apartments were never *that* messy. But the oktap – or rooftop shoebox flat – in Sangsu-dong where I last lived had been cheap, and too busy with his business trips to China, the landlord had never once raised my rent, which was how I ended up rotting in that small room for almost seven years. My belongings grew in number, and as I got busier, the rate at which I bought things eventually surpassed the speed at which I threw them out. The things I owned gradually spilled past the oktap's threshold, until every inch of the walls was covered.

On the flipside, Hana's place was the epitome of simplicity. She had one litter scoop, and one plastic bag for cat poop – everything in its rightful position. Apart from her books and CDs, she had only one of everything that served a function. Oh, if there was one thing that broke this principle, it was the fact that she had too many bottles of alcohol for someone who was living alone. Hana had so few clothes! What do you mean everything fits into that two-compartment built-in wardrobe?! How is that possible for a modern woman who's spent over twenty years shopping and living in a country with four different seasons?! Hana had been shocked when she saw my two-tiered rack come crashing down, overwhelmed by the weight of all my clothes. But when I recounted the incident to my colleagues, they weren't fazed. They simply nodded emphatically. 'Everyone has to deal with a broken clothes rack at least once or twice in their lives.' Fashion magazine editors may have very distinct personalities, but in that moment, we were united as one.

Hana's Samcheong-dong apartment, which had a breathtaking view of Inwangsan Mountain, was west-facing and could get quite hot. But she only had a small mid-capacity air circulator to tide her through the summer. She didn't have a fan for several reasons: there was no space for it, she didn't want to deal with maintenance and she couldn't find a pretty one. There were moments when Hana felt like a nun who preached non-possession (incidentally, she was later nicknamed 'Haemin Sunim of Mangwon-dong', after the Zen Buddhist teacher). My oktap measured about the same size as Hana's apartment, but as well as a similar air circulator and an air conditioner, I had a big fan *and* a small one. If Hana was a minimalist who only owned one of everything she needed, I was a maximalist who would use up the maximum allowance. If Hana was someone who took good care of her things and used them for a long time, I was the type to use my things carelessly, and if something broke, I'd tell myself I'd fix it, only to end up buying a new one to replace it. The earth loves people like Hana, while capitalism embraces consumers like me.

When two very different people – especially two people who treat their things so differently – decide to live under the same roof, there's sure to be conflict. After all, living in a house is the process of bringing new objects into a fixed space, using them, maintaining them and, finally, throwing them out. And if you're me, it's the process of bringing in new things, using them carelessly, never maintaining them and never throwing them out. Hana couldn't believe I didn't have a spot to put my nail cutters. Hers were always in the same drawer, from which she'd take them out when she needed them, and put them back once she was done. I had a pair in the bedroom drawer, a pair in the bathroom drawer, a pair in the catch-all tray in the closet, a pair in a basket in the living room . . . Whenever I needed to clip my nails, I'd reach out and grab the nearest pair. Why do nail cutters have to be confined to one single spot in a house when there's so much space? Plus, not all my nail cutters are the same. There's one that works smoother because I've used

I CAN'T GET RID OF ANYTHING

it for a long time, there's a bigger one that's great for cutting toenails, there's one that I got as a memento from my Tokyo trip and there's one that sits nicely in a flower-patterned amenity set . . . Hold on, I thought I had seven, where did the other three nail cutters go?

'A house reflects the inside of a person' . . . 'Houses resemble their owners' . . . I hated these sayings. Because if they were true, then I was someone with a complicated and sloppy soul, and I didn't want to believe I was that terrible. I'd always aimed to be someone whose mental space was much clearer than the physical space in which she lived. Not to mention, judging someone by the looks of their house felt to me as violent as assuming that someone's weight equated to their laziness. If a person who looked put together could be empty on the inside, then it was possible for someone to be systematic and efficient even when they were working in a chaotic house. Also, if a house reflected the people living in it, then Hana and I would be very different from how we were before. She would now be more complex and messy, while I'd be tidier and cleaner. Because the fact is my poor cohabitant has been patiently putting up with mountains of unpacked boxes, including ones containing a decade's worth of things from the job that I'd recently left.

The harshest thing that Hana has ever said to me is,

'Go ahead, live like a hoarder!' The accusation had hit harder than if she'd yelled, 'You're a damn fool!' precisely because there was truth to her words. I feared I would one day become a granny who's always lugging a hoard of trash behind her. But I'm trying my best to change, and that's what matters, right? While there are still plenty of items that I haven't got rid of, I'm better at controlling my spending. I've promised Hana I won't buy anything new before tossing out something old. Besides, these days I find more joy in paying off my loan than shopping. Rather than splurging on make-up or clothes, I prefer keeping my money as money, shopping for a new savings plan and buying the yen or dollar when it falls. Whenever I get the desire to shop, I recall those hurtful words. I still have a great number of books, CDs, vinyl records, cups, plates – and nail cutters – but I'm not going to die a hoarding grandma. I'm going to get along with and grow old with my cohabitant. But this maximalist still has a long way to go.

YOUR HOUSE IS LIKE A NEST

Hana   On 6 December 2016, 2 p.m., Hwang Sunwoo and I, both in our forties, became official home owners. That day, the December wind wasn't the only thing blustering through the living room. Stacks of boxes were piling up into mounds of chaos, and I wanted nothing more than to slip away into the lift lobby and disappear. *I'm going to run away and become a hermit!* Now why was I thinking that on a day that I'd so eagerly anticipated? Well, let's backtrack, shall we?

Ten months ago, Sunwoo invited me to her place for the first time. I was shopping for a bottle of wine and flowers when she texted: *My house isn't in a good state today. I'll invite you over again some other day.* It was a cold winter day, and I was already quite far from home, so I replied, *It's whatever! I'll head over soon,* and made my way to Sangsu-dong. I was already near Sunwoo's place, but instead of allowing me to go up, she insisted that we meet at a pub. When Sunwoo walked in, her face was ridden with exhaustion. 'Really, you can't come over today,' she repeated, over and over again. She explained that she'd spent days spring-cleaning, but no matter how much she got rid of, her house was still an irreparable mess. She'd thought it'd be ready by today, but she'd been sorely mistaken. Over skewers and beer, I insisted that I was fine with a bit of mess and begged her to invite me up. By then, we'd already talked about living together, so it was important that I saw how she usually lived. Thinking back, Sunwoo had come over to mine plenty of times, and whenever she did, she'd gasp, 'My house isn't like this at all . . . This could never be me!' Anyway, there was no changing my mind. I'd spent days looking forward to meeting her cats.

Feeling sorry for inviting someone over on a cold winter's day and then cancelling, Sunwoo eventually conceded. I was thrilled. We passed a cafe and a salon and came upon a neat building at the end of an alley. After climbing up four flights of stairs, we took the steel stairs up to the spacious roof which was covered by a thick layer of white. *It snowed?* I wondered inwardly. Turns out, the faint moonlight had made it hard to see, and what I'd thought was snow was in fact heaps of white rubbish bags. They covered the entire roof like a gorgeous blanket of snow . . . is how I'd like to think of that night. Sunwoo hurried me past the front door, denying me even a peek of the veranda. There I stood, at last, in the house where Sunwoo lived.

I met Goro and Youngbae for the first time. Unlike my timid cats, Goro and Youngbae were prime examples of lap cats. They strutted up to the entrance with curious eyes gleaming: *Who is this tiny human?* Goro was huge and Youngbae was tiny, but they were equally gorgeous. I was glad to finally meet the cats in person, and even gladder to be in the house of my long-time Twitter pal whom I found super cool. Sunwoo's house was cosy, very much like a nest. The living room/kitchen was filled with books. Just from one sweeping glance, I noticed some titles that I owned, and a few that I'd been meaning to read. *Similar reading taste? Check!* But those weren't all the books. There was a pile in her bedroom too next to a crammed collection of CDs and vinyl records (*Similar music taste? Check!*), which was next to a mountain of clothes, bags and jewellery (*No overlaps here*). Practically half of her bedroom was cluttered with things. In the bathroom, there was shampoo, conditioner, face wash, body wash, body scrub, body lotion, body butter, soap, hand soap, face masks, nose packs and tweezers – five of each on average. I say 'on average' because there were some things (body lotions) that she had twelve bottles of. Later, I found out that what I'd seen were only the things she was using, and that she had a separate stockpile of unopened products. Her little bathroom was stuffed. So stuffed that her towels were strewn everywhere because there was no space in her cabinet.

To summarize, Sunwoo had a lot of *everything*. Like a crow that collects shiny things, Sunwoo liked collecting all sorts of things, so much so that you couldn't see the floor of her house. Not to mention, as the editor of a high fashion magazine, she was always receiving free gifts. I'd later thank Supreme Court Justice Kim Youngran for enacting the Anti-Corruption and Bribery Prohibition Act which put a cap on the flow of gifts. Sunwoo's house was not exactly small for one person, but there was barely any space to move around. That was why it felt like a nest. I quite liked it initially. I thought it reflected her vibrant and charming personality, and I had fun poking around and looking through her knick-knacks. That evening, we had a small cake and wine, and chatted about how our houses were complete opposites.

Back to 6 December 2016, 2 p.m., cold wind biting my cheeks. As I stood there in the house where I would be living with the charismatic Hwang Sunwoo, my mind spun. *How did I not see this coming ten months ago? The evidence was right in front of my face! The trash bags on the roof! The house where I couldn't go two steps without bumping into something! What was I thinking bringing all of that into my life? Clearly I wasn't thinking straight!*

THE BIRTH OF DOBBY

Hana After a wonderful first visit, I started going to Sunwoo's more often. At the time, I was giving weekly copywriting lessons at Hongdae Sangsangmadang, and after two hours of nonstop talking, my throat would be begging for a pint of beer. I would walk over to Kushimura, a skewer restaurant, and meet Sunwoo for a beer or two (or three or four) – it became our routine. Reluctant to put an end to our conversation and laughter, we'd go to the convenience store to get the cheapest four-pack and head up to hers for another round of drinks accompanied by good music. Some nights I'd fall asleep in her house. On those occasions, Sunwoo would let me sleep in the next morning while she headed off to work. I'd wake up at my own time, clear last night's mess, and while I was at it, do a bit of tidying-up. It was nothing, really, but when Sunwoo returned in the evening, she'd gush over the cleanliness: *I thought I walked into the wrong house! It's never been this clean!*

There's an old movie called *I Wish I Had a Wife*, starring Sul Kyung-gu and Jeon Doyeon. And a 'wife' was what Sunwoo needed. Even when I was only just a follower on Twitter, I had a hunch Sunwoo didn't have the time to take care of her home. London, New York, Venice, Maldives – she was always somewhere on a business trip. She was the first to check out all the new places in Seoul, had meetings with all sorts of people, was at every concert or music festival, and if she was free, she was jogging along the Han River. If Sunwoo were a man, people would fawn over how capable she is, and in the midst of showering her in compliments, they might say something like, 'You should hurry up and find a wife to take care of the house,' or 'It isn't a bachelor pad if it's not a bit messy!' Yet, subconsciously, people always expect women to do well at work *and* take care of their homes. 'Is this how a woman's house should look?' they'll nag. No one ever says, 'You should hurry up and find a husband to take care of the house.' But no matter who you are, juggling work and the household is no easy task. A person can only pour themselves into their work if they have someone to fulfil the role of the 'wife'. That role can be fulfilled by anyone regardless of gender. It could even be a part-time housekeeper.

I, too, loved travelling and going out with friends, but unlike Sunwoo, I found joy in taking care of my home. If something that I considered barely any effort could lighten her burden, I was happy to do it. And as a fellow woman who was inspired by Sunwoo's accomplishments and drive, I wanted to show my support and cheer her on. Besides, I was always well compensated with Sunwoo's wonderful cooking.

With Sunwoo's permission, I became her official housekeeper. The first time I stepped into Sunwoo's place, I'd been surprised by the massive tangle of LAN cables that even her cats had to jump over to go in and out of the bedroom. I rolled up those cables nicely, and using cable clips, fastened them to the walls as inconspicuously as I could. Wielding my trusty screwdriver, I inspected the cabinets and drawers and fixed up any wonky handles. There was a hole in her bathroom sink – probably because she had dropped something heavy into it – so on the day I had an excuse to get her a congratulatory gift, I bought her a new sink and found a contractor to install it. I threw out everything that had gone out of use or was hopelessly glued together. There must've been about ten boxes of faded printouts and flyers, twenty broken umbrellas and a thousand dried-up pens. I replaced her old rubbish bins, dish rack, cutlery trays and towel rack, and reorganized all of her storage boxes. Leaning against the stove were two vacuum cleaners, which she always had to move out of the way whenever she wanted to make ramyun. I picked one lucky machine and gave it a spa day, unclogging the hair from its brush and replacing its batteries, and threw the other one out. It wasn't like there was any space to vacuum anyway. Lastly, I tackled the stove. With detergent and a sponge, I eradicated the greasy history of all the meals Sunwoo had cooked.

They say to live every moment like it's your last. Sunwoo's refrigerator was proof that the woman lived by that quote. If there was a sliver of space between the milk and ham, that was where she'd chuck the beer before slamming the door shut. She never spared a thought for her future self, who would have to open the fridge, poised to catch whatever was going to tumble out. The day I cleaned out her fridge – with permission, of course – I found a box of expensive chocolates. The chocolate lover in me rejoiced until I saw that it was three years past its expiration date. I could go on for ever about Sunwoo's fridge, but I'll spare you the horror and skip to the finale: the excavation of something dark, slippery and . . . curious – a head of cabbage that'd been relegated to the deepest depth of refrigerator hell by Sunwoo's *carpe diem* attitude.

When Sunwoo was on a long business trip to New York, I dropped by often to look after her cats. During that time, I took on my biggest project yet: cleaning up the forbidden veranda. Left untouched for six years, the space had been hijacked by a surprising number of shoes. OK, it wasn't *that* surprising. Sunwoo had every type of shoe, but among them, she had about fifty pairs of trainers including brand-new ones which she'd received as gifts before the Kim Youngran Act was enacted. Again, shout out to Kim Youngran. I spent two whole days mopping the veranda, rearranging her shoe racks and throwing out broken shoes. When Sunwoo returned from her trip, she reacted like one of those people who'd received a surprise home make-over. That day, in her sparkly clean kitchen, she made me the most delicious pasta.

Now that I'm writing this, I realize what I'd done was not 'barely any effort'. But I enjoyed making the house feel a little fresher, roomier, and watching Sunwoo's face light up when she returned to a clean home. Sunwoo called me 'Dobby', the house elf from *Harry Potter*. One day, she gifted me a pair of socks. The gesture is supposed to give Dobby freedom, but this Dobby slipped on her new socks and went back to scrubbing the stove.

WHEN TWO BECOME ONE

Hana   Back to me standing in front of the horrific mountain of boxes. Sunwoo was overseas that day, so I was the only one there to guide the movers. But there was no space to set anything down. Reluctant to part with any of her furniture and things, Sunwoo had lugged her entire oktap into our new apartment. Judging by the overwhelming quantity of her things, it seemed everything she owned was only meant to be used until *this day*. And by 'this day', I mean the notion of a big day where one's life dramatically changes due to a grand event – marriage, for instance – and their 'real' life trajectory begins. But in life, there's no such thing as a 'real' trajectory. Some people think of their school life as a temporary, transitional period of preparing for university. But as Yeongju would say, our school life is one whole, definite chapter in our story. Likewise, there are people who see their singlehood as a period of marriage preparation. Nowadays, as people are getting married later, that period of singlehood can stretch and eat into future plans. As such, treating that period of single-hood as the prologue to one's 'real' trajectory means living in limbo for a long time. Sunwoo, who hadn't known if she was going to get married, had spent a long time living like that, and it just so happened that as she was about to rethink her life, she met me.

And so, the things that Sunwoo had collected over her period of limbo flooded into our new house. They were strewn all over the floor, not only because there was not enough storage space for them, but also because Sunwoo had yet to go through everything and decide what to keep or throw out. She'd been too busy before the move, but I'd also boldly declared what would be my famous last words: 'Don't worry, I'll help you sort things out.' Previously hidden inside cabinets and drawers, the egregious quantity of belongings exceeded my estimations. It felt like I was stand-ing before the royal tombs in Gyeongju. Crying on the inside, I finally felt the full magnitude of welcom-ing someone else into my life.

Before moving in together, Sunwoo and I had gone on a week-long trip to Iceland with another friend. I wondered if our living arrangement was like Iceland – the meeting point between two astronomical-sized plates. While we were similar in many ways, our differences were much greater and starker. We were complete opposites, especially when it came to the great wave that we'd formed over the course of our lives – our daily habits.

Old habits die hard, especially if they've been formed over forty years. And when it comes to habits, there is no such thing as right or wrong, and not everything can be solved simply by coming up with rules to follow. When I helped Sunwoo with chores in the past, it was out of pure goodwill, and something that I did as and when I liked. But ultimately, the responsibility had always lain with Sunwoo. And so, although I disagreed with the way she organized her things, I never got upset. But now that her mountain of crap was eating into *my* space, reality hit me like a brick: I was looking at the topography of Sunwoo's forty-year-old habits, and I'd have to live with this monstrous wave.

Sunwoo, of course, was sharing the same horror.

THE ART OF FIGHTING

Sunwoo   Living well is fighting well. Differences in perspectives and conflicts are non-negotiable in life. For a long time, I had the wrong idea about fighting. I'd thought myself unconfrontational, and believed I should strive for a life without conflict. Whenever I saw people going at each other, I'd wonder, *What could possibly make someone that angry?* And if I ever found myself teetering on the brink of a fight with my partner or a friend, I would calmly excuse myself before things got heated. Alone at home, I'd ruminate, keep myself busy and wait for calm to return. I'd feel relieved if the matter was brushed off and forgotten, but if a person were to cross the line repeatedly, I'd slowly distance myself from them and eventually never see them again. Instead of expressing my disappointment or frustration and hashing things out, I kept in my heart a logbook of every letdown and judgement.

When I first heard the English phrase 'cry me a river' in a song, I scoffed at the idea of someone crying enough to fill a river. Initially, I thought the phrase meant something like, 'Go ahead, let it out,' but later on, I found out that it meant, 'Cry all you want, I don't care.' Anyway, just as there are people who can fill the Han River with their tears, there are people who can rage wilder than a tornado. Hana is a perfect example. There's an episode of *Friends* where Ross freaks out after finding out that his colleague had eaten his sandwich. His livid roar is cross-cut with a scene of New York pigeons flapping away in fright. Hana's outbursts would be followed by her own stock video of an exploding volcano. My short-tempered cohabitant herself has written about the countless times she'd fallen out with her friend Yeongju – their twenty-year-long friendship had always amazed me. That was, until Hana and I started living together, and I went from being a mere observer to the person she was always trying to unfriend.

We fought a lot. In fact, in the middle of writing this I'd almost started another fight by asking, 'So what *did* we fight about?' We fought because I had so much crap yet refused to throw out a single thing. We fought because I took for ever to put my laundry away, and because I'd come home late the night before we were supposed to go on a trip together. The number of things that I wanted to keep and the number of things she felt a person should have; our tolerance for how messy a house could be; the amount of effort we'd put into tidying up the house the night before a trip – we differed in every aspect. Each little difference became fuel for our fights, and it seemed like the rumbling floor between us would soon cave in. What was worse, the *way* we fought led to even more fights. Whenever a storm came, I'd run to my room to take cover, but Hana would throw open my door and yell, 'You can't just go to sleep at a time like this?!' Sure I can. When I was a kid, I'd always go to sleep and wake up feeling better.

Later, I learnt that the way I dealt with conflict was due to what psychologists called an avoidant attachment style. People like me tend to phrase things carefully or beat around the bush instead of saying things outright, and though we appear independent and composed in the face of conflict, we're actually trembling with fright. Fearing disappointment, we pretend not to care and write our problems off as trivial. I didn't avoid fighting because I was mature, but because I sucked at fighting. And if I ever got hurt, I could always retreat into my cave and sleep it off. But not any more. When you get into a fight with someone you live with, there's nowhere to run. Now that my back was against the wall, I had no choice but to face my problems straight on. No choice but to fight.

Hana and I still slip up in our words and actions. Our habits and principles still clash. And we still cross each other's boundaries sometimes. But we no longer fight so often. I've learnt that my biggest mistake is taking everything as an attack and jumping straight into defending myself. While my intention is to explain the thought process behind my actions, all the other party hears are excuses. And in my self-centred desperation to clear my name, I neglect the most important thing: acknowledging the hurt I've caused.

I've since mastered the art of fighting. Step one, apologize sincerely and as quickly as possible; step two, verbalize exactly what I've done wrong; and step three, assure the other party that their feelings are understood and valid. It took a year of living with somebody before I learnt these basic steps. In Korean, the phrase 'cutting water with a knife' is used to describe the brevity and impermanence of marital fights. I suppose the same words can be used for squabbles between friends. Hana and I would make up as if we hadn't bickered at all. Perhaps the mere act of slicing through water solves more than we think.

I wonder about the purpose of fighting. Is it to wield my best weapon and end my enemy in one swift blow? To crush them so that they can never get back up? I think I fight to forget the other fights I've had with the person I live with, the person with whom I'll continue to live. I fight to carve out a pathway for our emotions to flow. I fight so that harmony can always find its way back to us.

People can be happy alone, but as long as others are coming in and out of our lives, we must make an effort to maintain each other's peace. Hana and I may be stuck in an endless cycle of disappointment and forgiveness, but we will never stop pinning our hopes on each other. We will always be there to give each other another chance. I know that this constant battle is healthier than fragile peace.

THE GREAT TEFAL BATTLE
AND MY BIRTHDAY FEAST

Hana   In the days after we moved in, Sunwoo had to stay in the office until late, and so I took it upon myself to clean the house. I worked tirelessly, eager to see our house in its full glory, and to welcome my hard-working cohabitant into a neater and cleaner home each day. But soon it felt like I'd become Sisyphus, rolling his boulder up a hill. There was not enough storage space, and there were too many things that I couldn't throw out or move without permission. Not to mention we now had four cats in total, all expressing their anxieties in different ways. (There was also twice as much poop and pee to scoop out from the litterboxes.) I tired quickly and lost my temper several times a day.

As people who'd lived alone for so long, we owned many of the same things – TVs, microwaves, gas stoves, etc. Whatever we had two of, I gave one away.

But then I came upon two Tefal electric kettles. They were the same model, but one was unnecessarily big and clearly had been abused by its careless owner. Thinking that my smaller and newer kettle would serve us better, I texted Sunwoo: *Can I throw this out?* To my surprise, her reply was: *Isn't it more convenient to have a bigger one?* I wrote back: *One litre of water is more than enough to make two packets of ramyun.* My phone dinged. *The big one's good for filling up my heating pads.*

I recalled watching an episode of a marriage programme. When asked what she and her husband fought about, a woman answered, 'Just the smallest things, really. Like when he takes off his socks and balls them up.' In a thick Gyeongsang-do accent, the counsellor said, 'Between couples, no problem is really *that* small. They may start off small, but they start to pile up into something bigger, and that's when you lose your mind over balled-up socks. When a cup is filled to the brim, one additional drop of water could make it spill over.'

The same applies when you're sharing your most private space with someone. Since we moved in – or perhaps even way before that – my cup had slowly been filling up, and that giant Tefal kettle was the final drop of water. I lost it. *I've spent days wrestling with all this crap and you can't even let go of a damned kettle?! The house is in this state because you won't throw out anything!* My mind was flooded with not only the past couple of days, but also all the times I'd gone over to clean, tidy and fix up her place. Pushed to my limit, the gladness with which I'd volunteered to do everything morphed into frustration and rage. I hadn't expected anything in return, but perhaps in doing so, I'd unwittingly placed a burden on both of us.

Starting off strong with, *Go ahead, live like a hoarder!* I bombarded Sunwoo with enough messages to fill a diss track. Our dream house had turned into a hell hole. And in that moment, it seemed like my future was ruined. Enraged by the sight of the giant kettle, I chucked it under the sink and slammed the cabinet door. Sunwoo didn't respond to my messages. When she came home from work, she went into the room that we use as our closet, shut the door, and stayed there. I fell asleep angry. The next morning, Sunwoo emerged from her room holding two rubbish bags, eyes puffy from crying. I felt terrible but couldn't bring myself to apologize. Once she left for work, my calm returned and I resumed my duties as Sisyphus.

Sunwoo's boss said this about married life: living together with someone is communal living. The best partner isn't someone whose lifestyle matches yours, but someone who is willing to put in the effort to create a lifestyle with you. With the latter, any conflict can be resolved. That night, when Sunwoo returned from work, we spoke honestly about our grievances and made up. The giant Tefal kettle got to stay. It wasn't the real problem anyway, just the final straw.

When we first started living together, our differences constantly drove us up the wall. We'd scream and cry (Sunwoo said she'd never heard someone shout as loud as me). Two years later we barely fight. We've learnt to let go of the desire to control the other. Instead, we've painted a shared vision of our home, and have made clear to each other the space that we want to live in. Attempting to change each other only led to fights, and it was an impossible task to begin with. Working together towards a common goal, however, that's the team spirit needed in a group setting. While living with Sunwoo, I've let go of my obsessive need to tidy, and I've grown to be comfortable with a bit of mess. I've also come to think of some clutters as little habitats that contain their own life. On the other hand, Sunwoo has reconsidered the way she treats her belongings, and thanks to that, our house has maintained its balance.

A few days later, it was my birthday. As luck would have it, Sunwoo was also done meeting her deadline.

The house felt light. That day, I had the biggest birthday feast of my life. Sunwoo filled our table with enough dishes to make it wobble – my favourite flower crab, beef seaweed soup with shrimp, oysters, little meatball fritters, salad, greens and, to top it off, a bottle of Veuve Clicquot. I couldn't believe that she'd prepared everything by herself. Whatever Sunwoo lacked in the cleaning department, she made up for by being a pro chef. Every dish was fantastic; we got tipsy and enjoyed the first party ever held in *our* home.

INTRODUCING OUR CATS

Haku

Female
2006

Twenty-nine-year-old Hana's first cat. She was found on a rainy day, sitting in a box at the foot of someone's door. Shabby as a young kitten, Haku grew up to be spellbindingly beautiful. She's slender and must be handled with care, given that she's extremely sensitive and afraid of everything. But timid as she may be, she's full of curiosity and gets herself into trouble. Her name was taken from her first encounter with Hana, in which she had shrieked at her: *Haaak! Haaak!* She had then proceeded to ravage Hana's arms in scratches. Two whole months would pass before she let Hana pet her, but she's since become a lap cat, the cuddliest of the four. She won't let other strangers touch her, though. In fact, she won't even show her face.

Tigger

Female
2009

During a trip to Cheonsu Bay, Hana fell in love with a kitten striped like a tiger. She was told that she could bring the kitten home, but the owner had a last-minute change of heart. When Hana returned to Seoul, she couldn't stop thinking about the striped kitten. Then one day, at Hongdae Station, she came across a kitten identical to the one she'd fallen in love with. She was sitting in a box, put up for sale by someone who seemed mentally unstable. Hana quickly borrowed some cash from a friend, took the kitten home and named her Tigger. Tigger is a scaredy-cat, but she likes going on walks. In the old apartment, she'd open the windows on her own and disappear for a few hours before coming home. She's a chubby kitty whose belly is nearly touching the floor. Like Haku, she hides away from strangers.

Goro

Male

2008

Goro grew up in Yeouido Park until, one day, he approached Sunwoo's friend meowing, asking to be rescued. Unlike the other cats, Goro's life as a kitten remains a mystery. He's quite big, and like Puss in Boots from *Shrek*, he's got huge droopy eyes that melt hearts. He doesn't run away from people, and whenever a repair person comes over, he'll sit and watch or go through their toolbox. He looks like an angel, but get too close and he'll sink his teeth into your arm. He may be the only boy in the household, but he's got the girliest meow.

Youngbae

Female
2011

A strategist and a go-getter. The youngest of the four, Youngbae is the smartest and most agile. She's named after Sunwoo's favourite member of BigBang, Taeyang, whose real name is Dong Youngbae. While the others are street cats, also known as 'Korean shorthairs', Youngbae is half Abyssinian. The only cat born into a home surrounded by people and cats, Youngbae's got a strong personality and demands to be pampered. She's somehow learnt how to go potty in the toilet, a testament to her cleverness and eccentricity. She'll walk around the house meowing like a talkative friend, but won't let you hold her. She always looks like she's quietly scheming.

OUR TOES LOOK ALIKE
BUT ARE NOT THE SAME

Sunwoo The first musical that I paid to watch was *Cats*. I saw it in London, a trip that I'd painstakingly saved up for. All of the firsts that I experienced on that trip waver precariously in my mind, probably because they've been muddied by a mix of unmet expectations, poor execution and disappointment. *Cats* is one of the world's longest-running masterpieces. But at the time, I didn't have the experience I needed to enjoy the show fully. I was clueless not only about musicals, but also cats. I still remember clearly the beginning of the musical, just before the curtains went up, when the actors – I mean, cats – pranced towards the audience, their tails brushing against us.

Throughout the performance, I kept thinking, *That's all? When do we get to the important bit?* I was expecting the cats to combine powers to save a human in peril or a love triangle to unfold between the three main cats. But there was no such drama. All the cats did was gather in front of their patriarch, Old Deuteronomy, and decide on who among them should obtain a brand-new life. The audience was introduced to different cats who took turns sharing their stories. The first cat sang, then the next cat sang, then two cats sang a duet while they danced . . . Already weary from all the travelling, the sound of the English language lulled me to sleep, and soon, all the furry creatures on stage started to look the same.

Last winter, Hana and I saw a poster advertising the Seoul production of *Cats*. I was surprised when Hana said she hadn't seen the musical. She'd travelled all around the world and watched a show in every city, yet she hadn't seen the most famous musical?! I immediately booked us two tickets for the first show. By then, I'd racked up fifteen years of experience as a cat mum, and had found the perfect companion to watch musicals with. A companion with whom I scoop up chunks of cat poop every day.

One is fine, two's all right, I guess . . . But four's a bit too much, isn't it? Those had been my thoughts when I looked at my friend with four cats. Before I knew it, I'd become her, aka someone who constantly hears, 'Isn't four a bit too much?' If someone were to ask, 'So how did you end up looking after four cats?' I'd tell them, 'You know how life doesn't always go as planned? That's especially so with cats.' I had two cats of my own, but once I moved in with Hana, that number doubled. Plans are useless against fate. Thinking back, I didn't choose my cats, my cats chose me. In that sense, I suppose every meeting between a human and a cat can be called an accident. It's like being hit by a swinging boulder, except the boulder is a warm ball of fur. Or should it be called religion? Because since I've devoted myself to my cats, my life has been changed for good.

I'd been nervous to show Mum into our new home. *Two cats covering you head to toe in fur isn't enough? You had to get two more?!* Her nagging voice ringing in my mind, I hadn't dared to tell her that my cohabitant had two cats of her own. Thankfully, Mum spent a pleasant couple of days at ours and got along well with Hana. She left without finding out about the two extra cats. Having sensed a stranger's presence, Hana's cats had hidden in her room the whole time.

'You've got four cats at home, haven't you? I know all about it.'

Mum found out the truth after reading Hana's book, *The Art of Relaxing*, in which there's a chapter titled 'The Four Cats in My Life'. In any case, it's unlikely that Mum would ever get to see Hana's cats. The Samcheong-dong Kitties, Haku and Tigger, are always too shy and timid to show themselves to strangers (it feels weird to say 'your cats' or 'my cats', so Hana and I group them by where they grew up). On the other hand, the Sangsu-dong Kitties are more curious than wary. Whether it's the air-con repair person or a new friend, they'll come up to sniff them or dig around in their bags.

While it may seem like our cats can be divided into two categories, Shy or Not Shy, they're all different in their own ways. Haku, the oldest of the four, is the most sensitive and timid, and would jump at the sound of her owner's sneeze. If you hold out a hand to her, she'll back away. But then she'll flip on to her back and signal with her eyes for you to approach – a big tease, that one. She likes it when you run your hand firmly over every single bone in her thin body, and she'll stay snuggling in your arms until a loud sound from outside scares her away.

Tigger, the second youngest, is round and fat, and also a scaredy-cat. Once she warms up to you, however, she'll never stop asking for affection. Whenever I'm on the sofa, she'll come up and rub her face on me, stick to my side and whine if I stop patting her butt. Like a Hollywood star, she *knows* she's deserving of love and attention. She's the only one who appreciates an outdoors adventure, and once injured herself while frolicking atop hanok roofs.

The second oldest, Goro, is more like a big dog. He's got a round face and plump body, and likes sleeping at the foot of the bed or on top of the speakers with one foot sticking out. People who come to our house for the first time always say, 'You sure he's not a dog?' or 'He's as big as two cats put together!' Goro is the type to plop himself down on a stranger's lap, but if he's irked, he won't hold back a nip or scratch.

Last but not least is the baby of the bunch, Youngbae. She has so much energy and spends most of the day in a state of hyperactivity. She'll open the drawer where we store cat supplies and take out a toy to play with. If talkative cats are smart, then Youngbae is a genius. If she were a human, perhaps talking to her would drain us of all our energy. Hana and I always joke about how we are going to enroll her in KAIST, Korea's top research university.

Having four cats means living with four very different personalities. It's like having four pieces of clothing with their own design, colours and materials. In order to take good care of them and love them, we have to pay attention to their differences and treat them accordingly.

A Chinese colleague of mine, Wu Ye, said this to me once: 'China has a population of 1.3 billion. There are over twenty provinces, each with their own unique culture. Yet Koreans like to say, "Chinese people are like this and that." I can't bring myself to speak like that about Koreans. The friends that I've met in my ten years of living here are all different.'

It's easy to generalize what you don't know, what is distant or what you don't hold affection for. Who cares if we're lumping them together or equating them? But when it comes to the things we love, even the smallest difference is treated as special. That uniqueness becomes precious and means something to us. While living with four cats, I've come to understand the quirks of their kind, yet I always refrain from starting a sentence with 'All cats . . .' If there are a hundred cats in the world, then I believe that all hundred of them have different personalities. 'It's all the same' has now become a phrase that I can't and won't say – when it comes to cats, at least. One musical alone can't capture the eccentricities and differences in every cat in the world. Our household's version of *Cats* would have no dramatic plot twists or climax, but the characters alone promise a riveting story.

WE BECAME A BIG FAMILY

Hana　　　　People are seldom surprised when you say you live with a cat or two. If it's three cats, they might be slightly awestruck – 'Ah, really?' – but four cats, and you're sure to elicit a gasp – 'Whoa! Seriously?'

Even when I lived alone with my two cats, I only thought of us as a single-person household. My cats never answered when I talked to them and, more often than not, the house was silent. Besides, whenever my cats got hurt or came back from an appointment at the vet's, I'd always end up crying myself to sleep. But as soon as we became a W_2C_4 family of six, I knew for sure we were a big family. Whenever I opened the snack drawer, our four cats would approach meowing, stirring up noise in the kitchen. Sometimes when the cats teamed up with their siblings, shifted their territories a little, or stared each other down as they figured out their new dynamics, Sunwoo and I would fret over what to do to ease their anxieties. This was something we hadn't thought about. I was indifferent about getting scratched by the cats I had previously lived with, but felt bitter when I got swiped at or bitten by my new furry housemates. There were more than a few instances when I petted or hugged one of Sunwoo's cats before learning their temperaments, and was strictly punished with a bloody scratch. In those moments, I couldn't help but feel hurt, as if I'd remarried into a family where the kids lashed out, 'She's not our mother, she's just some lady!'

It's been over two years since we became a big family. I don't get bitten now and our cats don't fight as much any more. 'Your cats' and 'my cats' have become 'our cats'. This year, all six of us have been in and out of the hospital. Both Sunwoo and I took turns getting surgeries, and she got an extra eleven stitches after injuring her ankle. Our eldest cat, eleven-year-old Haku, was admitted to the vet for a dental procedure and has since fully recovered, while recently, our second eldest cat and the only boy, Goro, had surgery.

Compared to Haku, Goro's symptoms were much worse. Despite having had kidney stones removed in the past, he began having trouble going to the bathroom. We kept an eye on him but one Sunday, we found blood in his pee. Thrown into panic, Sunwoo and I combined forces to squeeze his tubby body into a crate and rushed him to the twenty-four-hour vet. I drove while Sunwoo sat in the passenger seat, hugging the crate. Poor Goro was petrified and his urine stank up the car. The monsoon rain poured relentlessly as we arrived at the hospital and throughout our consultation. I couldn't think straight. A few stones had appeared in Goro's bladder, almost clogging it completely. He had surgery the next day. While he was in recovery, Sunwoo and I visited him every day. It was heart-breaking seeing him lying in his box-shaped ward. Since big Goro couldn't stop himself from unsheathing his claws before the nurses and doctors, they'd wrapped his paws in bandages. Whenever he had an itch on the back of his neck which he couldn't get to because of the large neck collar he was wearing, he'd knock his bandaged back leg against the collar weakly before giving up. The sight of him so listless with an IV and catheter tubes dangling around him made me cry. Shortly after he was discharged, his condition took a turn for the worse, and we rushed him to the hospital again. Every day was torturous. Thankfully, Goro's health stabilized after his second surgery, and he's now at home, getting better by the day. Sunwoo and I have never been more grateful to have each other. It's nice knowing that when that day comes for the first cat to cross the rainbow bridge, we won't be facing grief alone.

As the saying goes, 'The tree with many branches shakes the most in the wind.' Large families experience double the happiness and double the pain. Then again, don't they say, 'Sadness shared is halved, while joy shared is doubled'? With a family this big, it's inevitable that we'll face many troubles. But I trust we'll see every last one through together. That reassurance is perhaps the best part about having a family, regardless of how that family is formed. I know we'll lean on each other, and that our joy will continue to double as we go through life's ups and downs.

WHAT I INHERITED FROM MUM

Sunwoo　　　　The opening scene of any movie is typically dedicated to introducing its main character through their appearance and actions. If I were to have my own biopic, my story would begin in high school. A sprightly schoolgirl nearly misses the school bus. Though the journey is short, she doesn't waste a minute, napping until she has to get off. The camera follows her as she skips towards the school gate. It focuses on her hefty backpack before zooming in on her even heavier tote bag. In it, there are two thermal lunchboxes for lunch and dinner, a hot flask and another lunchbox packed with fruits to snack on. That's right, I was the kid with the biggest lunch. I was always hungry, I ate a lot and my mum provided the fuel that fed my appetite. During a time when cafeteria lunches didn't exist and self-study sessions in the evening were compulsory, Mum had to prepare two meals for me to take to school. She would wake up a couple of hours early just to whip up something for her sleep-deprived daughter.

Back when I lived at home, I would wake up to sounds coming from the kitchen. A knife thwacking against the chopping board, soup gurgling in a pot or the sizzle of oil – these sounds, so vivid, would seep into my dreams. The smell of food would waft into my room, and at that age, I hated the feeling of my nose stirring awake before the rest of my senses. But now, if I were to wake up to see a table laden with food, I'd hop right out of bed. Leaving home and living alone represented morning after morning of waking up to nothing.

My mum, Han Okja, has spent her entire adult life cooking for other people, having married my father, Hwang Jin Gyu, who is the oldest of eight siblings. Every year during Seol, Chuseok and the two major jesa ceremonies of the year honouring one's ancestors, she'd fulfil her duties as the eldest daughter-in-law by going to the supermarket and returning with massive bags of groceries. She'd spend the whole morning preparing a feast all on her own, and when the festivities were over, she'd send off her guests with iceboxes filled with meat and sikhye, a sweet rice punch. *I've tried making kimchi myself, but it just doesn't taste like yours, unni. Sister-in-law, your siraegi soup is way better than our mum's!* For a long time, I'd thought of these compliments as empty words used to keep my mum in check. Until the tenth anniversary of my dad's passing, whenever I saw Mum preparing for jesa and cooking food to put on the altar, anger would rise up inside me. I believed that the glorification of home-cooked food underscored by the pretext that 'nothing beats Mum's cooking' only made things more difficult for mothers. It made mothers who were good cooks busier, and burdened mums who couldn't cook with guilt. Regardless of quality, why couldn't my aunts and uncles contribute a simple dish or order from a restaurant to lessen Mum's workload? But I'm one to talk ... I'm the one who's benefitted the most from my mum's cooking prowess. Every time I go back to Busan, every meal is carefully planned to include my favourite flower crab soup, braised ribs or stir-fried octopus, and my gut is forced to work overtime. That's Mum's idea of wholesome child rearing.

The weekly phone conversation between a mother and daughter from Gyeongsang-do can be summarized in three questions. *Have you eaten? What are you eating these days? Should I send you something good to eat?* Our brief phone calls have since grown longer. Because while I used to tell Mum not to bother, I've started to ask her for things. *Hana really likes the braised lotus root you sent last time. Would be nice if we had some chonggak kimchi.* Once I started, I couldn't stop adding to my list of requests. When I eat alone, efficiency and convenience are my top priority. Alone, I can make do with a boiled egg, an apple and a sweet potato, or throw a packet of instant rice and curry into the microwave. Funnily enough, humans are always more diligent when it comes to doing things for others. If I'm eating with someone, I'll make sure there's a soup on the table and at least a hot and a cold dish. Since Hana and I moved in together, I cook and eat at home a lot more. Cooking is a breeze when your cohabitant does the dishes and restores the chaotic kitchen to its original state. Even on late nights when I've been held back at the office, I like to de-stress by making a soup for the next morning. Cooking is my creative outlet and playtime, and it's a way of knowing that I'm taking good care of myself. The food that Mum sends supplements that sense of assurance.

At work, I'll wonder if Hana, who's at home alone, has eaten, if she's starving herself or if she's lazy and has made instant ramyun *again*. I'm starting to see it now: for Mum, cooking for family isn't a sacrifice. It's a form of expressing her love and concern; it's the joy of flaunting her skills; it's the challenge of managing and commanding a kitchen; it's a means of communicating with her aloof children. The more mouths Mum has to feed, the more her world expands. That world has come to include my cohabitant, Hana.

Now, I'm the one asking Hana the same kind of questions: *Have you had breakfast? What are you having for lunch? What about dinner?* I've inherited my mum's caretaking DNA. There had been days when I'd fought with Mum – over what, I cannot remember – and on those days, I'd leave my lunchboxes untouched. How had Mum felt then? When I think about those times, I could bury my head in shame. Perhaps my level-headed mum had simply thought, *Your loss.* That was just how proud she was of her own cooking.

THE TRICK TO GETTING
WELL FED

Hana   A friend who studies saju, or Korean fortune telling, once told me that food is written in my destiny. True enough, I've got a lot of friends who are chefs. Some by profession, and some who simply find joy in cooking for and feeding their loved ones. Among friends I'm known as the 'best person to cook for' and when I used to drop by Yeongju's for dinner, her mum would gasp, 'Is Hana a psychic or something? She always shows up when I'm making crab for dinner!'

How does a person who can't cook at all eat so well? Well, everyone, today I'll be revealing my secret on how to be well fed. All you have to do is . . .

Look like you're *really* enjoying the food.

I'm not telling you to pretend even when something tastes bad. But when you think about the effort that's gone into the dish before you, it's impossible not to lick your lips.

Contrary to popular belief, the most well-fed people aren't the ones who are good at critiquing food. The way I see it, there's only one case in which someone has the right to judge another's cooking: when they've paid for the food themselves. Cooking for someone is a noble act that stems from pure goodwill. It's a highly cumbersome task; the work of preparing all the ingredients, chopping them up, cooking them this way and that and, finally, arranging them nicely on a plate. That food enters our body, becomes our blood and flesh, and keeps us alive – what more could we ask for? When you eat with a grateful heart, everything tastes delicious. It's a simple law. Here's another: you must express your thanks in words *and* by doing the washing-up. In fact, the urge to do so should come naturally.

Just from scrolling through Sunwoo's Twitter, I'd never have guessed that she was a chef. She was definitely a foodie, but was always going out to have fun, and given her individualistic personality, I didn't think she would enjoy making food for others. But what d'you know? Every time I went over to hers, she'd make me something yummy. She wasn't afraid of difficult ingredients like crab and octopus and could whip up a delicious pasta or bibimguksu with whatever she had in the fridge. She was also a pro at making all sorts of Korean soups, greens and seasoned dishes. Always up for a challenge, she liked testing out new recipes and often succeeded on the first try. Once on a winter day, Sunwoo invited Mr Cheol-Day Star over for stew. Hearing that beer would elevate the taste, Sunwoo poured a generous amount into the pot. Alas, the stew came out too sour. *How's she going to salvage this? I guess even Sunwoo the Great has to fail sometimes*, I thought. But with no intention of giving up, Sunwoo quickly made a few delicious anju for us to snack on, and while our guests and I drank in the living room, she stayed in the kitchen working on her stew. At last she emerged from the kitchen and placed a pot of stew on the table: *Ta-da!* We cleared the pot in no time. Sunwoo had succeeded after all!

How lucky I am to have a cohabitant who's so generous, and I'm not only talking about portions. Every time we have guests over or host a party, the kitchen is turned upside down. Sunwoo's not a delicate chef, so it is up to me to deal with the aftermath. I've mentioned that offering to do the dishes is the key to being well fed, but the truth is, I *enjoy* cleaning. It thrills me to transform a culinary warzone into a showhouse kitchen. I work my way through the

piles of dirty dishes, stack them up nicely, give the oil-
and sauce-stained tiles and sink a good scrub, sterilize
the drain, replace the linens and sharpen the knives,
so that the next time Chef Sunwoo's in the mood to
cook up a feast, the kitchen will be good to go.

Even if food is written in your destiny, if you want to
be well fed, you have to put in the work.

CHRISTMAS GIFT EXCHANGE

Hana   On our first Christmas together, I gave Sunwoo a small gift along with a small favour: I Marie Kondo-ed the deluge of T-shirts overflowing from our shared wardrobe. Marie Kondo is a Japanese organizing consultant and the author of *The Life-changing Magic of Tidying*, which started an international cleaning frenzy. Around the time when Sunwoo and I were becoming closer, she'd confessed to me, 'I want to be tidier, but I don't know where to start.' When I mentioned Marie Kondo's book, she exclaimed, 'Ah! I have it!' Then her voice fell into a sad mumble. 'But it's probably lost somewhere . . .'

Sunwoo has a lot of things, but above all, clothes. She likes putting together new outfits, but can't bear to part with her old items. I remember the time I went to Sunwoo's oktap and witnessed a clothing avalanche, the collapse of her clothing rack which she called 'the king's wardrobe'. She assured me that this didn't happen often. When we dashed over to hold up the broken rack, I felt for myself the true weight of her shopping addiction. Later, Sunwoo went to the super-market to get a new king's wardrobe, and filled it up with clothes again.

The KonMari way of organizing T-shirts is to fold them up and place them vertically in your drawer. By filing your shirts, your drawer won't break, and you'll be able to find any T-shirt at one glance. Sunwoo had so many T-shirts that some of them had to be stored in the drawer below hers – mine. Sunwoo loved how tidy the drawers looked afterwards. The task wasn't a hassle for me. I had a relaxing time folding clothes, and was glad to be complimented.

Sunwoo and I do trades like this all the time. Living alone, there can be many chores that we dread, and things that we want to do, but don't have the time. With a cohabitant, so many things can be offset. Everyone has things they're naturally good at and can accomplish with ease. Whenever I fix a broken table lamp or take apart the electric fan to wipe down the blades, Sunwoo gasps, 'You can do that?!' But that's my reaction when I watch her cook. Sunwoo can come back from work past midnight, and still make two different stews before she leaves for work the next day. And she does it so that I don't have any excuse to skip meals. Worried she might be stretching herself thin, I'd told her to stop, but she replied casually, 'I'm telling you, cooking is relaxing and fun for me.' As someone who always makes more than she intends, Sunwoo doesn't like cooking for herself because of the leftovers. It seems she's happy to have someone who will gobble everything up. Just as I'd been shocked to see her clothing avalanche, perhaps Sunwoo would've rounded her eyes at my empty fridge. Being able to take care of yourself is admirable and respectable. But doing things for others adds joy and zest into our lives.

NEW YEAR'S DAY

Sunwoo   I invited Ari and Hanseong over for lunch on New Year's Day. The couple had just moved into the apartment two floors below us. In my invitation the night before, I'd confidently declared, *It's not a hassle at all! There's no big difference between two and four portions of tteokguk.* But I'd soon eat my words. When I clambered out of bed the next morning, it was already way past noon. What's worse, I dug through my fridge to find only enough rice cakes for two. I'd invited my friends in the hope of showing them a good time, but it seemed I'd be making them bring groceries and twiddle their thumbs while I scraped together something edible. After tasking my sous-chef Hana with garnishing the egg and cutting up the dried seaweed, I added kelp to the soup and crushed the garlic. I stir-fried lean beef and some soup ingredients in sesame oil, seasoned the pan with soy sauce and garlic, and brought the soup stock to a boil.

Then I left it up to the beef. My last secret ingredient is a splash of fish sauce. But really, it's all in the beef.

Ari and Hanseong arrived right on time, bringing two bottles of Gapyeong pine nut makgeolli wrapped in orange ribbon, cut fruits and my personal request – rice cakes. While I scrambled to make the tteokguk, I was suddenly glad that I had four cats. The ones who were less shy were hanging out around the guests, playing host. After adding in the premium rice cakes, whatever noodles I could find and a sprinkle of garnish, the soup was done. Plenty enough for five, it was delicious (or so I was told).

As we welcomed the New Year with milky-white tteokguk and makgeolli, we caught up with one another. I'd added some chamsora sukhoe from last night, and to my surprise, Hanseong knew exactly where and for how much I'd bought the parboiled conches. He'd thought of getting some himself. Since we'd run out of coffee the day before, Ari and Hanseong went downstairs to get some beans. We chatted some more over coffee before they left.

Unbeknown to our guests, Hana and I had got into a small fight the night before. We'd held an intimate New Year's Eve gathering with some friends, and after they left, Hana had wanted to count down to the New Year together by revisiting our past year. Mentally drained, however, I'd obliged with short answers and kept scrolling on my phone.

My excuse? By the time I'd done the grocery shopping, made the salad and sat down to start our mini barbeque dinner, it was already 9 p.m. Throughout the meal, I was in charge of the grill, and spent the night making sure that the meat didn't burn. As midnight approached, I was already sinking into a food coma. I smelled of grease and was utterly drained. My phone was flooding with New Year's wishes from younger co-workers, eager to celebrate with their seniors. And as much as I'd hate to admit it, I was addicted to social media. 'Can't you put down your phone for a while and just enjoy this sacred moment?' Hana sulked. I knew where she was coming from, but the greasiness and my buzzing phone won over. Sometimes, big moments in life require careful production and direction. Looking back, if we wanted to send off the year properly, we should've started the dinner at eight, sent everyone off by eleven, wiped the grease off the table, aired out the house and lit a few candles to set the mood.

After saying goodbye to Ari and Hanseong that afternoon, Hana and I started cleaning up. We cleared the dining table and did our daily chores – washing the dishes, setting the laundry, clearing the litterboxes and vacuuming the floor. And for the New Year house chores special, we replaced our two-year-old towels with new freshly laundered ones, and changed our toothbrushes, soaps, loofas, shower curtain, sponges and indoor slippers. By replacing all of these trivial, inexpensive commodities with brand-new ones, we kicked off the first of January feeling absolutely refreshed.

When the first day of the year was about to end, we switched on the radio. Hana's pre-recorded guest appearance on MBC Standard FM's *Wait a Minute* was about to come on. From the speakers flowed Hana's voice as she recited a brilliant excerpt from her essay collection, *The Art of Relaxing*, and spoke about how rather than setting up a definite plan, it was more important to keep asking ourselves, 'So, what now?' Hearing Hana speak with such eloquence on public radio, I was reminded once again that my goofy, pyjamas-wearing cohabitant had a cool and professional side to her.

As we hung out with friends and busied around the house, my mood gradually lifted. It may be tradition to light candles in the dark, reflect on the year's highs and leave behind our lows, but there is also something sacred in going about the ordinary – folding towels and trimming our cats' nails – that blesses us with a sense of stability.

Before we knew it, it was dinner time. Exhausted

from the socializing and chores, Hana and I decided to conserve our energy by going to a gisa sikdang, or cabbie's restaurant, for a cheap and simple meal. The neighbourhood was quiet, hushed by the wintry air. Once we left the apartment building and rounded the corner, the moon came into view. It greeted us, big and bright. Compelled by its radiance, we brought our hands together and made a wish. Putting aside the failures, mistakes and hurt from the previous year, we gazed towards the 365 days that'd been gifted to us; they were as full and complete as the moon overhead. That first of January, we thought of all the things we wanted to protect, and all the amazing things we wanted to accomplish.

It seemed the sacredness of the New Year had found us after all, just at a different time. It was then that I decided: come 31 December, we're going out to a restaurant to celebrate.

HAPPINESS IS BUTTER!

Hana   A while ago, two contractors came to install our new wall-mounted shelves. The deafening whirr of their hammer drill shook the walls, and there was dust flying all over the place. But just as we were praying to get the second shelf over and done with, the contractors said they couldn't finish the job. Apparently, the house's electrical system ran on a fuse box, and if the drill were to hit a wire, they could be electrocuted. Given the risks, we couldn't insist they carry on. But shouldn't they have checked to see if we had a fuse box beforehand, or warned us that, under some circumstances, installation might not be possible? The contractors then told us that we'd have to pay to return the shelf and left.

Standing in the middle of our chaotic living room, Sunwoo and I felt our souls slink out of our feet. The floor was strewn with furniture and things that we'd moved aside and bits and bobs of spare parts. There was no space for us to move around, much less clean, and just the thought of returning the shelf and shopping for a new one stressed us out. Sunwoo and I were *pooped*. When our stomachs started to growl, we roasted sweet potatoes and had them with butter. As we munched on our potatoes, too tired to even speak, Sunwoo – our resident butter lover – suddenly exclaimed:

'Happiness is butter!'

She laughed at her own sudden declaration, and I, too, burst into laughter. (Come to think of it, Sunwoo had once boasted, 'I never spread my butter!' By that, she meant that she only consumes butter in dollops.) Sunwoo's optimistic philosophy cheered me up, and I was glad to have a cohabitant who was so cheerful and pure-hearted. And since I was her cohabitant, I resolved to be just as cheerful and pure-hearted, and to pay more attention to the little things that brought me happiness.

Lee Youngju, owner of the lovely Manchun Bookshop in Jeju, once told me: 'There's a restaurant far away from where I live that sells the best hangover soup. Every time I'd go, I'd wonder, *When will I have this again?* One day, I found out that they do take-out, and since then, I'll always order an extra portion and store it in the fridge. It got me thinking, maybe happiness is a guaranteed future.'

To Youngju, happiness is a bowl of hangover soup waiting for her in the fridge.

There's a yummy sushi restaurant that Sunwoo and I love. We usually go at lunch for their discounted menu, but expecting a huge payment one day, I'd told her that dinner was on me and made a reservation for the next evening. On the day of our reservation, however, I opened my bank app to find only a miniscule deposit. After checking my contracts, I realized I'd remembered the wrong payment amount. I felt bad, but there was no time to mope – a delicious guaranteed future awaits! We enjoyed our dinner and I footed the bill wearing a smile. I thought of it this way: *I must be a genius! Booking a nice sushi dinner because I saw this disappointment coming.*

After dinner, we went to our favourite cafe, Mikaya,* and ordered coffee and a no-bake cheesecake, which tasted as incredible as ever. What is happiness? It could be butter, take-out hangover soup, a reservation for two at a sushi restaurant, or biting into a familiar dessert. I'm realizing now how much I talk about food. Perhaps food is crucial to Sunwoo's and my happiness.

---

* As of August 2024, Mikaya is permanently closed. We're sad that our favourite bingsu and cake place is gone, and would like to thank them for twenty wonderful years!

I hope you'll think about something that makes you happy, and if there's that something, I hope you'll try shouting, 'Happiness is ___!' Because in times of trouble, that phrase can help you bounce back quicker. All this writing has made me hungry. I wouldn't mind some sweet potatoes and butter.

FIVE-HUNDRED-WON
CONSULTATION

Sunwoo I'd never thought I'd face a career dilemma in my forties; one much worse than the one I'd faced in my twenties. Having graduated in the 1990s, a time when there was less competition, I'd had no problems landing a job. Recruitment was low during the IMF crisis, but the big magazine companies, at least, held open recruitments. I took a few tests, did an interview and secured an internship. Nowadays, new hires are expected to have accumulated work experience through apprenticeships or part-time jobs, and possess relevant skills like foreign languages, writing for social media or video editing. Instead of being given time and space to make mistakes and grow, they are thrown into impossible tasks that they must figure out themselves in order to prove their worth. Back then, I didn't have anything spectacular listed on my résumé – no foreign language schools, competitions or certifications – and the only thing I knew how to do was follow instructions. Past me wouldn't have gotten anywhere close to an editorial position. I owe the job where I'd stayed happily for twenty years to pure luck and good timing.

'Now that people are living up to a hundred years old, maybe marrying twice and changing careers thrice will become the norm,' Lee Hyeju, my colleague and editor-in-chief at *W Korea*, said to me once. As I approached my forties, Hyeju's words began to turn in my mind. I didn't care for marriage, but was it time for me to embark on that second career?

As a curious cat who loved hearing and writing about people's stories, being a feature editor at a fashion magazine suited me to a T. I was recognized by my colleagues, and every monthly issue rewarded me with a sense of fulfilment. But I worried, fearing the day the physical and mental stress would eat me alive. In the world of magazine publishing, ten days of the month were always spent in a frenzy trying to meet the deadline. I'd have to give up a weekend at least, and after days of working overtime, would spend one or two nights working in the office until the sun was up and the birds were singing. On days when I'd spent the previous night at the office, I'd come home and flop on to my bed feeling like I couldn't move or breathe. But after the following month's editorial meeting, a few off days would make me forget all about the insufferable nights until, without realizing it, the next deadline was on my arse again. My job was like a lover with whom I'd fight and make up. I'd freeze, then melt; cry, then smile. Amid the whirlwind of emotions, months flew by, turning into years. At last I realized I wasn't getting any younger, and thought I'd like to try a different pace of life. If you love someone, let them go – my job taught me this.

When I started my new job at Gentle Monster, I had two main concerns. One, so used to coming into the office late, I wasn't sure if I could be punctual. Two, working on Excel. Much to my surprise, I liked getting up early in the morning and having ample time to get ready, and my superior hated working on Excel even more than me. Even in my forties, I was discovering new things about myself, and learning that there was no use in making assumptions about others.

My new workplace offered a different rhythm of life, but it would take a while before I could dance to its beat. Notwithstanding reporting time and Excel files, I had to familiarize myself with new tasks, rules, skills and a new company culture; both my body and mind felt clumsy. A married friend of mine once said that visiting her in-laws feels like being adopted into a new home as an adult – that was how I felt at my new workplace. For months, I felt like a stranger who'd arrived in a foreign land, and must prove herself to the natives by using their language.

But what a relief! That at the end of each day, I would go home to someone who'd listen to my troubles. And as someone who had spent just as many years as me socializing and whose worldly insights I trusted, she dispensed the best advice. Likewise, when Hana was hosting on the radio programme *On This Starry Night*, she would share with me beforehand the concerns sent in by listeners, and we would discuss what advice she could give. The solutions that we came up with together were always better than the ones we thought of alone.

The phrase 'Don't put persimmons and pears on someone else's jesa table' means not to stick your nose into other people's business. That doesn't apply to me. We can't see the full picture unless we step back, and it is difficult to swallow things that are piping hot. While people may be good at telling others to take it slow or to leave, they somehow hesitate when it pertains to their own relationships. We all need a consultant. When I was thinking of leaving the job I loved, when I saw potential after a job interview, or when I have to practise a nerve-wracking presentation, I can always trust my live-in consultant to explore my options with me and guide me towards the right path. Easily excitable, there are times when Hana gets way too ahead of herself, but I've always got my stubbornness to rein things in.

No matter the circumstances, my consultant always has faith in me. Whenever I feel defeated, her belief that I'm fully capable, sensible and will always strive for a better version of myself gives me the support and strength I need to keep going. I, too, have the same faith in her. That's why I've agreed to write this book with her. I'm trusting her to guide me through the process. For her time, Hana charges me a special cohabitant rate of five hundred won per consultation. I'd be OK with paying a thousand.

WE LIVE IN DIFFERENT WORLDS

 *Hana*

Me: What's that sound?
Sunwoo: What do you mean?
Me: That crackling noise. It's quite loud.
Sunwoo: Really? I don't hear anything.

The sound was coming from a radio that wasn't tuned to the right FM. After switching off the radio, Sunwoo reminded me that at our last medical check-up, I'd received a hundred on my hearing test, while she, an eighty. It struck me then: not everyone has the same physical perception of the world. It seems that although most people understand that feelings are subjective, they think that physical senses are objective. But that's not the case. Everyone lives in the world differently. I have very good eyesight, while Sunwoo has a prescription of -5.5 dioptres. Without her glasses, my face appears as a round blur. Even with contact lenses in, her vision is still worse than mine. Whenever I saw water marks on the mirror or stains on the table, I used to grumble, 'Why can't she just wipe them off?' But that was because while I saw these blemishes so clearly, Sunwoo couldn't see them at all.

That reminds me. Last February, my friends and I went on a trip to Tongyeong. The air was still crisp but, located on the southern coast of the Korean peninsula, Tongyeong was a lot warmer than Seoul. We were strolling about when I burst out in awe, 'Whoa! The flowers smell so good!' Looking around, my friends asked, 'You smell flowers?' There wasn't a flower in sight. I thought I'd imagined the scent, but I looked up and saw a lone apricot tree standing on the edge of a cliff. Riding the wind, the subtle floral scent had reached my nose. My friends said I had a dog's nose.

The same goes for my sense of taste. I'd always thought of myself as someone who wasn't picky and didn't know much about tasting food; but there were times when I'd casually say something like, 'Ooh, did you put figs in this?' and the chef would say, 'How did you know? Only a tiny bit!' All in all, I suppose you could say I'm a *very* sensitive person.

I even have to wear earplugs to bed so I don't get woken up by my cat scratching at the door. My goodness! I'm basically a walking antenna. How does anyone live with me? *Could you lower the volume? What's that funny smell? What's that stain on the ceiling?* Imagine living with someone who won't shut up about every little thing. Japanese novelist Junichi Watanabe wrote a book called *The Power of Insensitivity*. He refers to 'insensitivity' as the power to let things go without obsessing over them. It's a good thing that I live with someone who has this superpower. Meanwhile, I've been trying my best to foster my insensitivity, but it hasn't been going well.

It took over forty years and a crackling radio incident before I found out I was a sensitive person. When I realized this, I recalled the time I found a book lying on the table titled *Sensitivity, a Weapon*. It belonged to Sunwoo, who was probably reading it to understand her very sensitive cohabitant. I related to many things written in the book and spoke about it on my podcast later on. Living with someone has helped me learn about myself. Our differences are much more obvious and we are constantly in contrast to each other. It is important to find joy in our differences and make an effort to stay true to who we are. In learning more about myself, my under-standing of my cohabitant expands. The reason we perceive the world differently is because we live in different worlds. That's why it's my job to wipe off the water stains. *Groans*

BUYING PEACE IN
THE HOUSEHOLD

Sunwoo 'When are you going to put away your laundry? You can't keep grabbing underwear or a towel from the clothes airer and leaving the rest there!'

When I started my new job, the peace that my cohabitant and I had maintained by doing our share of the chores started to crumble. Coming home late, I'd throw my bag on the floor, flump on to the sofa and scroll on my phone before dragging myself into the shower – the same pattern went on for weeks. I used to make up for my untidiness by cooking, but since I was eating all three meals at work, I couldn't muster up the will to go grocery shopping on the weekends. When I lived alone, I could let my laziness fester as much as I wanted, but in a communal space, the disintegration of rules affects everyone involved. It was no wonder that, after weeks of covering my chores,

Hana had exploded in anger. As I watched her go off, I sulked inwardly, *The house is big enough. What's the big deal about leaving out the clothes airer? If I take things off the airer one by one, it will be empty and ready to use when the next batch of laundry's done.* But don't tell her that.

According to a study from the Korean Women's Development Institute on the average time spent on chores in dual-income households, men spend an average of nineteen minutes per day on housework, while women spend two hours and fourteen minutes more. Nineteen minutes? Well, I suppose running a lint roller along the sofa while lying on it, soaking their plates in water before leaving them in the sink and tossing their dirty clothes into the laundry bag after showering would take a man nineteen minutes. If there's a world out there where I could come home and find dinner laid out for me, my shirt for tomorrow freshly pressed and the toilet roll replaced before it had even run out, I'd love to live in it. Then again, perhaps I would oppose that lifestyle. Because to me, there's something childish about an adult who will do anything to avoid housework. Actually putting in the work to *live* out your own life is part of what makes a person whole.

'Your peace of mind is worth buying.' My father

believes that if money can solve some of our problems, then we should let it. And so I took his advice. I
downloaded a housekeeping app and booked a cleaning service. But watching someone do the work that I'd
failed to do made me feel uncomfortable. Unable to bear
the awkwardness that first time, I'd helped the ajumma
clean. Now, when the housekeeper comes, I point out
the spots that need more attention, and excuse myself.
I still feel a bit ashamed of hiring someone to do my
chores, but it's hard to go back once you've had a sweet
taste of comfort. In fact, I might be addicted to the rush
of coming home to see a glistening floor.

'Leave the housework to us, so that you can focus on
what you love.' This is the housekeeping app's tagline.
No matter who you are, if you're able to do the things
you love, it is only right that you feel both grateful and
guilty that someone else is doing your chores, be it
your wife, mother, cohabitant or housekeeper. While
the ajumma works up a sweat in my house, I'm outside reading a book, meeting my friend or indulging
in a drink. Forty-five thousand won per visit, a hundred and eighty thousand won per month, the amount
spent on a shopping trip – that is how much it costs
to give my tired body and mind a break from the mid-
week chaos, and to restore peace in our home.

Here comes the plot twist. One day, I came home

slightly earlier to find that the housekeeper had left an hour before she was supposed to.

When I texted my friends about it, one said: *Maybe she saw two young women living together and thought she could take advantage of them.* Hana and I weren't exactly young, but I suppose the housekeeper had seen us that way because we weren't married and didn't have any kids. I'd left the house and always offered the housekeeper fruits and something to drink so that she could do her job without feeling pressured, but perhaps I'd come across as a softie in doing so. Whether we live alone or with a friend, it seems the world treats unmarried women the same.

THE WIFE AT HOME AND
THE WORKING HUSBAND

Hana   In Mincheol and Ilyeong's relationship, Ilyeong is the 'ahn-saram', the stay-at-home
wife, and Mincheol is the 'bakkat-saram', the working
husband. 'Saram' means *person*, and 'ahn' and 'bakkat'
mean *inside* and *outside*, respectively. Since I've known
her, Mincheol has held an office job, while Ilyeong
spends most of his time at home as a grad student.
As the person who looks after the house and packs
Mincheol her lunch, Ilyeong fulfils the traditional
role of the faithful ahn-saram. In Mr Cheol-Day Star's
home, traditional gender roles are reversed.

During a conversation with the couple, we talked
about the ahn-saram and the bakkat-saram of our
household, and easily concluded that I was the former,
and Sunwoo the latter. I was a freelancer who worked
from home, and Sunwoo had spent twenty years of
her life working in an office. Since that conversation,

we'd always joke: *Did my ahn-saram have a good day? Have fun at work, bakkat-saram!* Once, Sunwoo left the house saying, 'This bakkat-yangban's off to work!' The word 'yangban' means *nobleman*, which got me wondering: *Why is the person who goes to work considered to be higher in status than the person who stays in? And why does the term 'bakkat-yangban' exist, but not 'ahn-yangban'?*

The problem was, although I was the ahn-saram, I was staying in to *work* my freelance job. Still, because I was at home, the weight of the house chores also automatically fell upon me. Throughout the day, I would find myself picking up the trash, clearing the litterbox, vacuuming the floor, doing the dishes and folding the laundry. Something was off. The chores never ended, and as long as I was at home, I'd always spot something that needed doing and naturally became the main housekeeper. When Sunwoo came home from work, she'd throw her bag on the floor, chat with me, go on Twitter and then hit the sack. The next morning, she'd shower, dry her hair, get dressed and leave for work. It was up to me to pick up her bag, clear her hair from the floor and while I was at it, vacuum the floor and clear the litterbox – you get the idea. This went on for a while. At the start of living together, this problem was my greatest stress. For one, cleaning everything from the bathtub to the dusty shoe rack took for ever, and I was spending way too much time on housework. Two, notwithstanding the fact that my cohabitant wasn't the most detail-oriented person, my efforts, at best, could only ever amount to the house looking no different from usual. But if I were to leave the house alone for a bit, it'd turn into a mess right away.

Sunwoo was the type to leave traces of herself around the house. Think Hansel and Gretel. Even when she wasn't at home, I could always track her movements: 'Ah, Sunwoo took her pills here.' (There's a ripped medicine packet on the kitchen counter that she didn't throw into the bin right beside.) → 'Sunwoo wore contact lenses today.' (There's an opened blister pack on the sink. And a bin not more than a foot away.) → 'Huh, Sunwoo used the scissors.' (There are traces of something that has been cut, and a pair of scissors lying splayed out on the table.) → 'Looks like Sunwoo's picked a new book to read.' (The books that I'd organized are mixed up and there are a few lying on the floor.) Meanwhile, I was the type who couldn't start work until everything around me was spick and span. I would clean up my cohabitant's mess and, while I was at it, do the other chores. Moreover, given my strange proclivity for making sure that the kitchen was pristine, I was always exhausted before

I could even open my laptop. My problem as Dobby, the resident cleaning fairy and ahn-saram, was that I simply couldn't leave anything alone.

Perhaps it would've been fine if the bakkat-yangban earned the money while the ahn-saram managed the money and the household. But Sunwoo and I contributed the same amount to our living expenses. If we ran out of money, we'd top it up again, splitting the amount fifty-fifty. It just wasn't fair. But if I were to just 'leave it', as my bakkat-yangban cohabitant had insisted one too many times, our four-kitty household would fall apart, and it was I, the stay-in ahn-saram, who would have to drown in the mess. And so, I came up with two solutions. One: working outside. I found good conducive cafes and used them as my office. The trick to not doing housework is to not be in the house at all! Two: getting compensated. On weeks when I'd done most of the chores, I'd ask my cohabitant to pay up. Without a word of complaint, Sunwoo would send a token of appreciation. Once my labour became paid work, I instantly felt better. There's nothing sweeter than proper pay!

These days, Sunwoo hires a housekeeper to come in on the weekends. Guided by her personal philosophy, 'Anything that can be solved by money is no big problem,' this is her attempt at rectifying the chore imbalance. The first time the housekeeper came, I didn't know how to feel about watching someone older than me do the housework, so I escaped to Mincheol's. Claiming that she was fine, Sunwoo stayed in. But she eventually caved and helped with the cleaning. Too funny.

Just the fact that the bakkat-yangban is making an effort to fulfil her half of the workload puts my mind at ease. Besides, for an ahn-saram, a clean house truly is the best gift.

So to all the bakkat-yangbans out there: open your wallets!

BOOZY CITY GIRLS

Sunwoo   Here are some factors that determine a singleton's quality of life: clothes, food, shelter and . . . neighbourhood friends. A friend you can call up when you don't want to go home after work, but don't want to spend time with your colleagues; a friend you can meet for a quick drink, bare-faced and in your comfiest sweats; a friend you can ask out on a movie date on weekends when the house feels too quiet; a friend you can meet at the bike rental stop and ride around the park with. With a person like this within fifteen minutes of where you live, life feels kinder.

But if you don't have a friend like this, and would like to make one, you won't find them through blind dates. Don't get me started on dating apps. While apps can tell you exactly how far away a stranger is, it won't tell you how well they hold their liquor, how well they deal with loneliness or when they'll seek company, if they're looking for love rather than friendship, how often they work overtime, etc. Plus, it's rare that all these variables will align with what you're looking for. Finding a good neighbourhood friend is like searching for a unicorn. But guess what? I live with one.

Living with a good friend is essentially having a neighbourhood friend who lives zero metres away. If there's a new movie you'd like to see, you can ask if they're free right away, and if you're watching something on-demand, you can stay on the sofa and launch straight into your reviews. There are downsides, of course. Coming home to your best drinking buddy means you consume way more alcohol than before. I drink twice as often now: when I want to drink, and when Hana wants to drink.

When Hana and I moved in together, we married our bookshelves, just like in Anne Fadiman's essay, 'Marrying Libraries'. On the other side of the living room, we married our liquor cabinets. But while we sold or gave away our extra books, we left our alcohol collection untouched. Tanqueray, Hendrick's, Monkey 47, Bombay Sapphire . . . We can concoct any variation of gin and tonic, and have a collection of single malt whisky from different origins. I wasn't the biggest fan of cognac until I tried Hana's Hennessy and Camus XOs, which opened my tastebuds to a whole new world of whisky. Since we can't have hard liquor every day, we stock up our fridge with wine and beers for casual consumption. When Hana's mum, who was up-to-date with the latest Korean dramas, first saw our alcohol collection, she'd gasped, 'You two are boozy city girls, just like in *Work Later, Drink Now*!'

At some point, all my favourite bars began to disappear. These were places I'd go whenever I was too lazy to call up a friend, and wanted to unwind alone. There was one bar run by a friend of mine and others where I'd slowly become friends with the bartender and their regulars – those places were like old pals to me. Now that they're gone, the only bar that I visit is my living room. It is where my best drinking pal and I are the owners, the DJ knows our music tastes and only our favourite anjus are served. Once, Hana and I, both buzzing with alcohol and greedy for more, had debated on hitting a bar. But ever so candid, Hana yelled, 'No way! You can't get a woman who's taken off her bra to put it back on!' Laughing, I posted about this on my social media, and immediately Mr Cheol-Day Star called, offering to let us have some bottles of wine from their collection. Since I still had my bra on, I went downstairs to accept their gift. Our drinking session ended on a happy note. See how there's no reason for us to leave the house?

OUR RETIREMENT PLAN:
HAWAII DELIVERY

Hana   Are we Seoulites or Busanians? Since moving to Seoul, Sunwoo and I have spent more time in Seoul than Busan. At home, we use standard Korean with a sprinkle of Busan 'satoori', or accent. Being in the big city used to give us butterflies. 'Ah, Seoul's the best!' we'd say. We immersed ourselves in the big city and indulged in everything Seoul had to offer. But over time, we started to feel trapped. There was one thing that Seoul didn't have: the sea. The Han River couldn't replace the view of a boundless horizon.

And so when we were in Busan during the holidays, we'd take in the sea view and sigh, 'Ah, Busan's the best!' Cool in the summer and warm in the winter, Busan was a haven for two souls who were sick of the erratic Seoul weather and stifling Han River. As we gazed at the ocean, the questions tumbled out naturally: *Should we move to Busan when we're older? I was just going to ask you that. What will we do for work? We could open a pub by the ocean. Will we have energy for that? We could hire some younger folk. Or only work four days a week.* These conversations formed a vague picture of our autumn years.

When Sunwoo and I drink, we always put on music. I listen to quite a lot of music, but nothing compared to Sunwoo. She listens to pop, rock, jazz, classics – everything. But there's one niche genre that we both love: music that can bring out the flavour of our alcohol. Born only six months apart, Sunwoo and I grew up listening to the same songs. We're noisy when we drink. *Oh! This song! Well, if you like that, you'll love this. Whoa! I loved this song, too!* It always starts with one of us playing the music until the other says, 'This song reminds me of another,' and we'll take turns playing each other songs. This is why we have our own Bluetooth speakers; so that we can both be the DJ. Rather than music that requires our full attention, we prefer music that we can groove to. In fact, we get even more excited when it comes to our guilty pleasures. We'd always whisper a disclaimer, *Don't tell anyone I said this, but I* love *this song,* then, recognizing the intro, we'd squeal, *Oh my god! This!!*

One day I proposed an idea: how about we take turns posting a song recommendation every day? After considering different platforms, we decided on good old Twitter. Sunwoo was worried about staying consistent, but I assured her we didn't have to take things so seriously. I quickly opened my laptop and made us a new account. We came up with the name Hawaii Delivery (@hawaii_delivery). It was a phrase printed on a keychain that was lying on the table at that moment, and we thought it had a nice ring to it. In the bio, we wrote: *Curating a playlist for the oceanside cocktail bar that we'll open in twenty years.* We found a picture of a neon sign that read 'cocktails' and set it as our profile picture. Then, we made a YouTube playlist with the same name. The reason I'd rushed to start the project was because my manuscript was due soon. And as we all know, in the face of an encroaching deadline, people like to expend their energy on anything but the task at hand. And so, I uploaded my first song recommendation, Harold Melvin & the Blue Notes' 1975 release, 'Hope That We Can Be Together Soon'.

Since 28 February 2017, we've recommended a song a day. We'll cover for the other if life gets in the way, and we don't insist on a fixed schedule. Up until now, we've kept the account's admin a secret.

Hawaii Delivery isn't a total reflection of our music tastes. Excluding songs that are too solemn, quiet or noisy, we only upload tunes that people could dance to in a pub by the seaside. As it turns out, this simple routine has changed us. Through the other's recommendations, we've come to understand each other better, and by sharing a playlist, we always feel like we're together, passing the same time, even when we're physically apart. We are conversing, one song a day.

As of 27 January 2019, Hawaii Delivery has 7,063 followers and 667 songs on its list. We've got a couple of fans too. Our playlist proves its worth every time we put it on in the background while we clean, go on a drive or have drinks together. If you're reading this, I hope you'll look up 'hawaii delivery' on YouTube, and that the songs will stir up the image of blue waves, ebbing somewhere in your imagination. A while ago, the Hawaii Delivery duo went to Hawaii. We brought the keychain and took a photo to commemorate. Each time we add a song to our playlist, we dream of the seaside cocktail bar we'll open someday. And each time, at least for the duration of a song, the sea whooshes into our lives in Seoul. They say that picturing your future brings you one step closer to that particular future, and perhaps this is our way of preparing for retirement. Everyone has their own, whether it's annuities, real estate or investing in their children. We've chosen to curate songs. Whether or not our bar becomes a reality, we're having fun dreaming and reaping the profits.*

---

* We closed the @hawaii_delivery account in April 2021.

MANGWON SPORTS CLUB

Sunwoo   When Hana and I get hooked on something, the excitement rubs off on the other. One of our most recent obsessions was *Graceful and Gripping Women's Football*, an essay collection written by football fanatic Kim Honbi. More than just an avid spectator, the author writes about joining an amateur women's football team, running and scoring goals on the field, and pouring her heart and soul into the sport. Hana had read the book first, and trapped within the boundary of her enthusiasm, I myself fell in love with it. Together, we went around spreading the good word. I was thrilled to live vicariously through these women from all ages and backgrounds who were brought together by their love for football, who trained and competed together, who had both won and lost, and were ultimately motivated to win again.

Things are different now, but back in my day, women who weren't professional athletes were estranged from sports. We were encouraged to get a head start or hone our talents in other subjects, but PE was always treated as an extra-curricular activity that we just had to pass. In elementary school, the gym was ruled by boys, and whether it was at home or in school, instead of being allowed to run wild and enjoy their childhood, girls were expected to have self-control and be ladylike. In middle and high school, aside from preparing for the mandatory fitness test, there were no opportunities for girls to enjoy sports on a constant basis. Even now, I still wonder why dodgeball was the only sport that female students were allowed to play. Surely there were other games that didn't require girls to run away from a ball and sit out once they were hit, and that didn't engender a fear of white volleyballs. A game like, I don't know, football or basketball maybe?

Under such circumstances, many girls would only discover the joy of sports as adults. I spent my tumultuous twenties doing everything I could to avoid sports until I tried it out for myself in my early thirties. After suffering a paralysing sprain in my shoulder, I saw an orthopaedist who told me that I'd torn my rotator cuff. Wearing the most indifferent expression, the doctor dropped another bomb on me: thirty is the start of ageing and physical decline. *And here I thought my only problem was getting saggy!* The doctor said that to prevent future injuries, I needed to strengthen my muscles. So just as we would treat an illness with medicine or a jab, I started rehabilitative weight training. Ten years have passed and I realize now that if I hadn't hit that low, I would've drowned by now, without even realizing that the water was creeping up. No matter how late, it's a relief that I discovered the importance of keeping fit and the joy of using my body.

Having achieved the boss level of aloneness in my thirties, I enjoyed working out alone. Exercising was much more efficient when I could book a private session with a personal trainer, do my own weight training, or lace up my trainers and go for a run without having to match someone's schedule. But tennis taught me the value of putting up with a bit of inconvenience. The fun of serving and returning in a rally isn't something that I could do alone or with a machine. That high is only achievable with a partner who can move.

Although it's nowhere as serious as Kim Honbi's football team, Hana and I have our own sports club. The Mangwon Sports Club, or MSC for short. While I prefer to do things alone and in a swift ninja style, Hana doesn't mind the cumbersome work of bringing people together and possesses all the qualities of a good team captain. Besides, she was the woman behind *Catchball Weekly*, a club that met up in the Gyeongbokgung area to stroll around the neighbourhood or play catchball. The members of MSC are mostly friends in the neighbourhood, but they also include Hana's friends from Seochon and the good folks of the Frivolous Knowledge Club. (They've since rebranded as the Frivolous Foodie Club, a group that goes around trying out new restaurants.) We're all friends that can hang out whenever, but since we'd moved to Mangwon-dong, we figured why not take advantage of the neighbourhood's community infrastructure? The MSC's main activities include bowling at the Mapo Residents' Fitness Centre, renting Ddareungi bikes and cycling in the park and swimming at the community pool in Mangwon Hangang Park.

When familiar faces and our usual jokes are supplemented by movement, there are more reasons to laugh. We at the MSC may all be clumsy amateurs, but we teach and learn from one another. Through our swim meets, someone has learnt how to do flip turns, someone has learnt how to breathe freestyle and someone has learnt to swim underwater. Unfortunately, we've got a party pooper in the MSC – me. Due to my competitive nature, I may or may not have got upset over losing a bowling match.

One of the most useful skills that I've picked up

from my ever-so-zealous cohabitant is swimming. Shortly after moving in, Hana found out about the community pool just fifteen minutes away from ours, and signed up for a beginners' swimming class. Her first lesson was in February, at an ungodly hour in the morning and when the weather was still freezing. This was surprising coming from Hana, who would always mumble, 'All that for what?' whenever she saw someone exerting themselves. But she took up the challenge and stuck with it for ten months. For a while, Hana swam even when she was at home. She would look up swimming tutorials on YouTube, suffer in pain because pool water had gone up her nose, very maturely decline alcohol because she had a swimming lesson the next morning and practise her strokes by leaning against the wall or lying face down on the bench, kicking her legs. I bestowed upon her the nickname 'Mangwon-dong Tadpole'. After months of constant practice, the Mangwon-dong Tadpole mastered breaststroke, freestyle and backstroke, and eventually grew into a frog who could do butterfly. With no intention of stopping, Hana started to give swimming lessons to me and her friends.

As someone who likes to get things done lone-ninja-style and will mull over what she'll achieve next, I admire Hana's dedication to helping people improve and succeed. She's always genuinely happy for them when they do, too. Having inherited her schoolteacher parents' genes, Hana doesn't only have a nurturing heart, but is actually good at teaching. Last spring, we went on a trip to Hua Hin with four other friends. Only half the group knew how to swim. But after staying three nights at accommodation with a swimming pool, we all left Thailand as swimmers. One of our friends had experienced a traumatic incident in her childhood and didn't dare put her head underwater, but even she was gliding in the wide pool on the last day. Watching her, our hearts swelled with pride. We gave Hana a new nickname – a combination of her nickname, Tol, and the name of Helen Keller's mentor, Anne Sullivan: Teacher Tollivan! A month after our trip, it was Teacher's Day. The friend who'd learnt how to swim thanks to Hana bought her carnations and gave her a letter. *We love you, Teacher Tollivan.*

My fitness role model isn't among the hot personal trainers I follow on Instagram or any pro athlete. It's Hana's mum. 'Do you know where confidence comes from when you're old? Your stamina.' Hana's mum says this as someone who used to have a petite frame and fell sick all the time. Since her forties, however, she's been an active yogi and swimmer. One day, when she came to pick Hana and me up from Busan Station, she told us the story of when she successfully swam underwater for the first time. 'There was someone at the pool who could swim from one end of the lane to the other in just one breath. I thought it was the coolest thing, but it didn't seem like something I could do. Not properly anyway. But one day, I set my mind to it. I told myself I'd go only as far as I could, but the next thing I knew, I'd gone the whole way. All in one breath! My, what an incredible feeling. So don't ever doubt yourself and just go for it.'

I'm in my forties, and there are still so many sports that I haven't tried and muscles I haven't used. Just like swimming from one end of the pool to the other in one breath, there must be things that I find daunting, but can no doubt conquer. It's been ten years since I received that warning from my doctor and started exercising. I'd like to continue taking on all sorts of new challenges, and make the most out of my body for a long, long time.

It's true what they say. If you want to go fast, go alone. But if you want to go far, go together. Besides, having company means you won't get bored. My next goal is to play tennis with my friends from the MSC, but perhaps I should send Hana to some classes first, so that *she* can teach our friends.

MY PRIMARY GUARDIAN

Sunwoo   One of Hana's and my favourite novels, *Fifty People* by Chung Serang, is set in a hospital. Each of the fifty chapters is written from the perspective of someone different – a doctor, patient, carer or mortuary assistant, for instance – allowing readers a peek into the lives of those who live and work in a hospital. When I read the novel, I was viewing the complex and intricate workings of a hospital as a world that was alienated from mine. After all, healthy people don't think about their health. But one day in March, I found myself lying in a five-person ward, looking out the window down at the city smothered in fine yellow dust. I'd become a tiny part of a massive hospital.

As if we were at a rock festival, Hana and I crossed our hands together and took a photo of our matching patient–guardian hospital wristbands. The wards were all perfectly south-facing – a courtesy perhaps to the patients who were cooped up – and from my bed beside the windowsill, I could stare into the distance and watch evening descend slowly upon Umyeonsan Mountain. How long had it been since I spaced out and did nothing at all?

I was admitted to the hospital two days after I left my thirteen-year office job. The surgery was minor and only required a three-night hospital stay and three weeks of rest, but while I was working, I simply couldn't bear to take any time off. I recalled the famil-iar view of the sunset from my Nonhyeon-dong office. This new view from the ward and everything around me were unfamiliar, but nothing felt stranger than the person under the stiff hospital gown. Following the hospital's instructions, I'd taken off my accessories, contact lenses and my cute gel manicure. Without make-up and proper showers, us patients bore a vague resemblance to one another. Just a few days ago, I was in an office doing a job that only I could do, surrounded by magazines I'd poured my life into, and people who recognized my unique talents; I was proud to be that diligent worker bee who couldn't even bear to take a month off to look after her health. But now, stripped of the traits that define me, all I had left were my gender, my illness and a tag bearing my name.

'It'll sting a little. Deep breath in.' When I was told

I needed an enema before the surgery, I thought I'd be given laxatives to prep my bowels, just like when I did a colonoscopy. Little did I know, I'd be lying with my butt in the air, a needle stuck in my arse. The process went smoothly, thanks to the expedient and capable nurse. It almost felt like going to a bank to exchange currency. As I waited for the effects to kick in, a sense of degradation rose inside me. Given that I was just another one of the countless patients with the same minor illness, I understood the nurse's unfeeling attitude. Yet I felt bitter that she'd treated me as if I were invisible.

After the surgery, the rest of my hospital stay whizzed by. The anaesthesia wore off, and my aching body and painkillers kept me in a constant daze. For a few days, all I did was eat and go to the bathroom, and I realized how useless my wanderings on dignity and shame had been. Three times a day, the nurse came to take my blood pressure and temperature. After hooking me up to the IV drip, she would openly ask if I was farting OK. I'd been told that since I'd been put under anaesthetic gas, it was crucial that I did deep breathing exercises. Throughout my stay, Hana stayed by my side. She bought me a spirometer, an instrument with a plastic ball inside that I could move by blowing into a tube. Normally I could replace the jug on the water cooler by myself without breaking a sweat, but I was so weak from the meds and fasting that I could barely make the little ball in the spirometer float. Eating was a whole other issue. The hospital food was so well seasoned and nutritious that I would get it for take-out if I could but, regardless of taste, I couldn't stomach more than a bite. And while the running app on my phone had once clocked a distance of 1,200km, I couldn't walk without clinging on to my IV pole, and one short stroll around the hospital floor felt like a whole workout. As a big eater and an exercise junkie, and as someone who loved those sides of me, being a patient rendered me a stranger to myself.

Funnily enough, when I was well enough to leave the hospital, the sight of Hana packing up my things reminded me of the very first day we got here. Holding a backpack carrying my underwear, a shaver and slippers, Hana had exclaimed, 'I know we're going to the hospital, but doesn't it feel like we're going on vacation? I almost packed the selfie stick!' The memory elicited both a chuckle and a wince, for my belly was still weak. Though my hospital stay was far from a vacation, it wasn't totally unbearable thanks to Hana's company. On the day the surgery left me half-conscious from the pain, and whenever the nurse came in at dawn to check my vital signs, Hana was always there – a light sleeper, she would sit up from her narrow bed and be at my side, ready to assist. Once, as I watched Hana sleep with her back towards me, the steady rhythm of her snoring had pricked at my heart (I found out later that the snoring had come from the ajussi behind the curtain). Those uncomfortable nights would eventually become stories that Hana and I like to tell.

I will never forget how wonderfully Hana stepped up to the role of my primary guardian. In my weakest moments, she reminded me of all the half-marathons I'd finished. When my mind wasn't cloudy from painkillers, she entertained me with jokes. More importantly, she assured me again and again that this very farty version of me wasn't my entire self. It was only four days and three nights, but through it all, Hana held on firmly to me, so that I wouldn't disappear; so that I could find my way back to being me again.

WE ARE SONS-IN-LAW

Hana   Once, when Sunwoo's mother called, I shouted loud enough for her to hear, 'Eomeoni! Your yeolmukimchi was delicious!' Sunwoo's hand flew to cover her phone and she shushed me. 'Why?' I mouthed. She gestured for me to keep quiet, but her mother had heard my voice and so Sunwoo sighed, 'Ah . . . That was Hana. She said she liked the yeolmukimchi. Yup. That would be nice, but please, only just a bit. I'm serious, Eomma, don't send a huge box!' Later on, Sunwoo explained that her mum was the generous kind, and that her generosity was sometimes 'hard to handle'. I didn't think much of the incident until the next morning when I received a text from Sunwoo's mother: *I sent you some more kimchi.* When I got home and opened the giant Styrofoam box, I understood why Sunwoo had shushed me so urgently. The box was practically bursting with enough radish kimchi to feed an army, a variety of

179

banchan, ingredients for cooking and other goodies like misugaru, a traditional Korean multigrain powder that is often made into a drink. Our fridge was fully stocked. All this just because her daughter's friend had yelled something over the phone? I was grateful and amazed by her earnest generosity. (But Sunwoo was right, the enormity of that box was indeed hard to handle.)

My father has a small writing room right by Songjeong Beach in Haeundae-gu where Sunwoo and I like to have staycations. Whenever we go to collect the keys or borrow towels and any furniture we might need, the whole family, including my brother's, will gather for a meal. Fond of these rare family gatherings, my father knocks back drink after drink. While the rest of the family tells him off, Sunwoo accepts every drink he pours her, and is the only one who can keep up with his pace. Needless to say, my old man approves of her. He gushes over her kind and warm attitude, and the last time I went back home alone, he'd grumbled, 'But . . . why didn't you bring Sunwoo?' It seemed he thought of my cohabitant as a drinking buddy. When I told Sunwoo this, she burst into laughter: 'I kinda feel like a son-in-law!' Whenever we go out for barbeque, my parents never let Sunwoo hold the tongs. All she has to do to please my parents is eat the meat that they've placed on her plate, clink glasses with my father and be her silly self. And not foot the bill, of course.

The more I think about it, the more I realize how good Sunwoo and I have got it. If each of us were to get married, would we be this comfortable with our husbands' families?

I feel like sons-in-law are always treated well while daughters-in-law are expected to treat other people well. In fact, Sunwoo and I enjoy a much more comfortable status than a son-in-law – as 'the friend our daughter lives with', we are free to accept kindness and hospitality without feeling obliged to the other's parents. I can savour Sunwoo's mother's delicious yeolmukimchi without worrying about planning a filial piety trip or whether I should buy her a new home appliance to show my thanks. All I have to do is say, 'Tell your mum the food was great!' Sunwoo and I adore each other's parents. We're always happy to see them and are always thankful for their kindness. And that's probably because our relationship doesn't come with strings attached. Thanking our own parents, though – that's self-service.

A while ago, my mother broke her glasses. Luckily for her, Sunwoo works at Gentle Monster, the hottest eyewear brand, where all employees can get a certain number of glasses made for free. Sunwoo sent Mum a link to the website and asked her to pick her favourite. Mum, however, was hesitant because of the unexpectedly high price tag. After Sunwoo insisted, saying that she wasn't the one paying for it anyway, Mum eventually picked one, and even took a selfie wearing her new glasses to show her thanks. I wonder if my mother would've hesitated or been this grateful had she received the gift not from her daughter's friend, but from her daughter-in-law. Because things like this are considered a daughter-in-law's duties – but for a friend of one's daughter, it's seen as goodwill.

Goodwill – the word, to me, means 'from the heart'. A heart that precedes customs, familial relations, responsibility and duty; a heart that is truly grateful to one's friend's parents for bringing someone so precious into the world. A heart that wants to pamper the person who lives with their daughter. A heart that is shared by every daughter-in-law, son-in-law, mother and father, and mother- and father-in-law in this country. Having maintained the pure shape of that heart, it seems Sunwoo and I, busy munching on yeolmukimchi and meat, are winners.

A WEEK ALONE

Sunwoo   Once, Hana went away for a week. She'd gone to Jeju to give a lecture and go on a family vacation to celebrate her mother's seventieth birthday. In the ten months that we'd been living together, I'd gone on a few business trips and vacations, but this was the first time that *Hana* had gone somewhere and I was left alone. Just me and our four cats, in our big house. I was surprised when I caught myself trying to hide my excitement. Living with Hana was nice; comfortable. But it'd been a long while since I had some time and space to myself. Perhaps without realizing it, I'd come to feel like a married woman.

When asked by her husband of fifteen years what she'd like for her birthday, my friend Kim Seunghyeon said, 'For you to get out of the house and leave me alone.' As a married woman who lives with family and has to look after her kids, my friend didn't want clothes, a nice purse or diamonds – she wanted to be alone. Introverts recharge their batteries by staying in and being by themselves, but women with kids rarely have that luxury. Even if they're at home – a place of rest – they're always on their feet, doing things for others. Just as the rich get richer and the poor get poorer, people who live with family get busier. Back when I lived alone in a house where I had free rein, I thought it strange that someone would ask to be alone for a birthday gift. But not any more. I wasn't dying to have the house to myself, but it came as a nice surprise.

As soon as I came home from work that first night, I switched on the sports channel. Hailing from Busan, the city of baseball, Hana and I are fans of Lotte Giants, and we'll sometimes invite our friends over to drink and watch the game. But Hana has a baseball-related trauma. For over twenty years, she'd lived with her father, a baseball fanatic, and through-out that time, had been subjected to the insufferable din of baseball matches blaring from the TV. Plus, she hates how nasty baseball fans get whenever their team loses. But me, I like leaving the TV on and hearing the announcer's voice and rowdy cheers crescendo and fall according to the events unfolding.

That first evening alone, I binge-watched a Lotte Giants game, some other team's game and caught the highlights on a baseball news programme. The absence left by my cohabitant was filled by a sound that I'd missed.

It was just before the long Chuseok holiday, and my schedule was packed. I made plans with my friends, but mostly I was so busy with interviews and work that I'd come home drained and desperate to shut myself off from the world. Since my work involved a lot of talking, it was nice to steep in a bit of silence. I'd eat a simple dinner while I watched TV, feed the cats, empty their litterboxes, tidy up a little, and just like that, the days flew by. In the meantime, I got bored of all the baseball, and while I'd planned on taking advantage of my strict cohabitant's absence to wreak havoc, I didn't have the energy to go through with the mischief. Hana's house rules weren't exactly difficult to follow and having abided by them for a while now, I'd unwittingly fostered a habit of cleaning. After flying through a few simple chores, I spent most of my time lying down. With nobody bothering me or fretting over me, the air around me was always perfectly still. Just like it had been those twenty years. After a week, my hectic work schedule caught up with me, and I came down with a terrible flu.

On the day of Hana's return, I went to Gimpo Airport to pick her up. The bright display board was flooded with the word 'delayed'. A plane's faulty tyre had damaged the runway surface, and all departures and arrivals had been postponed. As I waited for Hana on a plastic bench in the arrival hall, I thought about how I'd changed in the past ten months, and about how my week alone was about to end. The presence of others naturally breeds inconvenience, which can sometimes be as dreadful as damaged tyres ruining a perfectly good runway. Without my cohabitant around, my week had gone smoothly, carefreely and efficiently. But there was one thing missing – laughter. I thought I'd got sick because of my heavy workload and busy schedule, but another hypothesis surfaced in my mind. What if my immune system had shut down after so many days of eating alone, of tension seizing my body and of living with my laughter button switched off? The trick to releasing stress, nervousness and anxiety is no big secret. Sometimes, all it takes is a little joke, some messing around, or a mundane conversation. Everyone needs someone in their life with whom they can talk about anything and nothing at all.

I spotted Hana's round face, blended in with a crowd of noisy middle-schoolers coming back from a field trip. I'm not usually a crybaby, but in that moment, I felt a sour ache in my nose. The person with whom I share silly jokes and pointless conversations was finally home.

THE QUEEN OF DESTRUCTION

Sunwoo   You might know Midas, the Greek god who turns things to gold. But have you heard of Hwang Sunwoo, the woman who destroys everything she touches? The title of my biopic would be *The Queen of Destruction*. I don't do it on purpose, of course. My nature is a recipe for destruction: I'm careless, impatient and on top of that, I'm strong.

Bad with both home organization and technology, I've broken many household appliances because I didn't know how to take care of them. When Hana and I moved in together, we both brought along our air circulators, but it wasn't until the end of summer that I learnt that electric fans had to be dismantled and cleaned before they were put away.

Or I guess I kind of knew, but summer was ending, and then life got in the way . . . Before I could touch that air circulator, it was already summer again. Under my care, many household appliances have had their lives cut short – may they rest in peace. My cohabitant has stepped in and got rid of the humidifier damaged by cat pee and the broken vacuum cleaner, but there are still a few dead laptops lying around the house. A person who breaks everything but can't throw out anything? Trust me, even I can't stand myself. Unlike me, Hana only buys what she needs and takes good care of her things. She's the type to read *The Way Things Work* for *fun*. Living under the same roof as Hana has taught me so much, but I doubt she'll say the same about living with me.

In the winter, we decided to get a portable heater. I thought a simple electric one would do, but Hana insisted on an oil heater. Apparently there was a big difference between the two, starting with the vibes emanating from real, flickering flames. True enough, the oil heater was incredibly warm. I was a bit worried about using oil, but all I had to do was be careful and remember to air out the house occasionally. I love our oil heater for two reasons. One, whenever we switch it on, our cats assemble, stretch out their furry limbs lazily and bask in its warmth. Two, the top can be used as a stove. Whenever we put a kettle on, swirls of steam transform our house into a romantic winter cabin, and roasting whole oranges douses the living room in the sweet-savoury scent of sweet potatoes. Speaking of which, sweet potatoes are my favourite thing to cook on the stove. All we have to do is wrap them up in cooking foil, leave it on the heater for thirty minutes and there we'll have it – the perfect hot treat to thaw the cold.

One evening, I was cooking sweet potatoes when I caught a whiff of something burning. I'd done a shoddy job of wrapping the sweet potatoes with whatever cooking foil we had left, and it seemed something had trickled through the cracks. Sensing that something was wrong, Hana asked, 'Are your potatoes all right?' I should've explained myself right there and then, but my human instincts kicked in, and I fudged an answer to cover my arse. Or perhaps it was my primal instincts speaking, desperate to protect my precious sweet potatoes. In any case, I lied. My plan was to eat my sweet potatoes, and scrape off the evidence before I got found out. But losing myself in my starchy treat, I forgot all about the soot caking on the heater, and thus, the Queen of Destruction's perfect crime went kaput. Before I could clean the heater in secret, I was busted. 'Did you keep this from me even though you knew all along?' According to Hana's recount of the incident, my pupils had been darting left and right.

Without a word, Hana wetted a kitchen towel and began scraping off the soot. I tried to take over, but I wasn't just the Queen of Destruction any more. I was someone much worse – the Queen of Destruction *who had lied and betrayed her cohabitant's trust*. And so I couldn't do anything except berate myself inwardly as I watched poor Hana wrestle with the heater. When her tireless scrubbing didn't work, Hana sprinkled baking soda and vinegar over the soot and went into the bathroom to brush her teeth. The constant rhythm of her brushing sounded angry to my anxious ears. Fair enough. After a while, Hana emerged from the bathroom and returned to the heater again. This time, her scrubbing made an egregious sound that grated against my ears. That moment lasted an eternity.

If you ever burn something in the kitchen, remember this: baking soda and vinegar. Thanks to the power of chemistry, the soot was wiped away, and I, too, was cleanly forgiven. I'd learnt another life hack! As punishment, I had to wash the rags and was barred from using the heater to make food on my own. And so the case of the burnt sweet potatoes was closed. As the weight in my chest lifted, I imagined a parallel universe in which I lived alone. In that world, there is no clean cohabitant. I am sitting by myself, munching on sweet potatoes. The top of the heater is caked in soot, and I let it build up until I decide to throw out the heater, cutting its lifespan short. Alas, in that world, my winters are shabby and bleak.

GOOD THING WE
LIVE TOGETHER

Hana   When I lived alone, the *crack* of my furniture expanding or the sound of footsteps outside my door would wrest me from sleep. I'd get up to double- and triple-check that I'd locked the door and windows, and make sure that both my cats were fine before going back to bed. But by then, I'd be wide awake. The more I forced my eyes close, the more my mind swarmed with useless, anxious thoughts. Every mistake that I'd ever made, even the smallest ones, would come back to haunt me. I'd worry about messing up the next day, and then I'd remember a spot I'd missed while cleaning. As sleep slipped further and further away, the thoughts in my head swelled: *How long will this relationship last? How long will I live? What will happen to my cats if I die?* According to a neuroscience book that I'd read, negative thoughts exist in a part of our brain that works like a closed circuit; instead of disappearing, they can go on and on like a hamster wheel. What's worse, that hamster wheel can grow. On those nights, I wouldn't sleep a wink, and I'd spend the next day trudging around with puffy eyes and weariness scrawled across my face. 'How I wished I had someone who would just *sleep* in the spare room at night,' I lamented to a friend. The fact that I was fully responsible for my home's safety was unsettling and exhausting. It felt like I was constantly using up unnecessary energy – a boiler running throughout all four seasons.

One of the best things about living with somebody is that they act as a powerful attention diffuser. There's no need to constantly be on my toes, which significantly reduces my anxiety. Something as simple as having someone to talk to while cutting up fruits can chase away tension and melancholy, and as these little interactions become a constant in my life, I become more relaxed and stable. Just knowing that there is someone else in the house brings me peace. As a matter of fact, they don't even have to be in the house. Knowing that someone will be coming home is enough. I mentioned this in the beginning, but for a long time, I loved living alone. I could spend a whole day by myself without switching on the TV. But it's sort of like travelling alone – it is only when you go on a trip with someone that you realize that all your solo travels had been spent in a state of nervousness, tension and constant alertness. Since living with Sunwoo, my insomnia has magically vanished. I sleep well – perhaps *too* well – and so does Sunwoo.

Having a human alert system is nice, but there are times when my cohabitant is a blaring red alert. Sunwoo is the Queen of Destruction, always bumping into things or spilling stuff everywhere. You've heard of 'golden retriever boyfriends' – men who have a cheery, naive personality – well, I live with a golden retriever girlfriend. But my careless pup doesn't just break things, she gets into accidents and worries me sick. Once, when cleaning out the litterbox in the veranda, Sunwoo stood up, rammed her back into the water faucet and crashed straight to the floor. As a safety measure, I cut a hole in a tennis ball and stuck it up the tap. I did the same for all the sharp corners around our house, a project which I called 'Wilsoning the house', inspired by the brand of tennis balls I used.

A fully Wilson-ed house, however, can't guarantee that the Queen of Destruction won't get into accidents outside the house. When we were vacationing in Jeju, Sunwoo left early one morning to train for her half-marathon on an olle trail. Just when I was starting to worry that she'd been gone for too long, I heard a knock. I was about to open the door, but the person on the other side was holding on to it firmly. Through the narrow crack, Sunwoo meekly warned, 'Don't freak out.' At last she swung the door open, revealing herself, a bloody mess covered in mud. Horrified, I burst into tears. The wet path that Sunwoo had slipped on left her with a nasty gash on her knee and several other minor cuts. For the rest of our trip, we started our mornings by hobbling to a hospital in Seogwipo to get Sunwoo's dressing changed. I'd thought that was a one and done incident – we weren't running around like careless children, after all. But no. Sunwoo would later fall off a bike and cut open her knee, bang her ankle against the toilet door in the office and get eleven stitches, etc. The moment I forget about past incidents, the red alert blares, and once again, I'm sobbing from shock. I'd never thought that I'd meet an adult so clumsy. Nor that I'd cry like a baby every time my friend got hurt.

Accidents aside, Sunwoo makes the most reliable attention diffuser. I love people who are always moving around; their vigour, and the energy that colours their cheeks. As my golden retriever – oops, I mean, cohabitant – bumps into things while she does her daily stretches, puts on her leggings to go on a run, hops over to the fitness centre to do ballet, or does yoga, her energy rubs off on me. Being near her lively energy was one of the reasons I wanted to live with her.

Living with an active cohabitant and near the out-stretched Han River have changed me. While I still live and breathe books and enjoy my slow strolls along the alleyways, I've found joy in swimming and biking. Before I had to quit swimming, I'd made it into the advanced class where I learnt the butterfly stroke, and cycling thirty to fifty kilometres along the Han River is nothing to me. So you see, pure will isn't everything! Who you live with and where you live can make a huge difference.

Now pause – I've got a story for you. I was cycling along the river when I received a call from Sunwoo. Putting down the brake, I picked up the phone.

'You're biking? Whereabouts?' Sunwoo asked.

'Yup,' I answered, looking around. The sun had set and the only thing I could see amid the darkness was a neon sign across the river that read 'Chung-Ang University Hospital'. 'I'm near where we found out we were overweight . . .'

Sunwoo and I are not only serious about exer-cise, but also food. At our first health check-up after moving in together, Sunwoo and I were told to watch our weight. We took it as a sign that we'd been eating, moving and sleeping well. Though perhaps we should've done less of the former.

Sunwoo is not only physically fit, but also a naturally conscientious person. And in your forties, your physical health and conscientiousness are directly linked; you can only be as conscientious as your body allows. The morning after having drinks together, I'd always peel myself off the bed, take a hangover cure and resume a foetal position, but Sunwoo would hop out of bed early in the morning and leave for work. On weekends, she'd get dressed, do the chores and even go out for a run. I started to get self-conscious – in a good way. On mornings when I'd shuddered at the thought of getting out of the covers, I'd drag myself to the swimming pool. And on days when I wanted to laze around and pretend my manuscript didn't exist, shame would nip at me and I'd open my laptop. Living with someone you respect is infinitely more motivating than living with a chronic nagger. Eventually, the things that you do for the sake of leaving a good impression on your cohabitant manifest into something worthy. My improving fitness and growing list of achievements blossom into pride and motivation. I'm grateful that my cohabitant is also my role model.

Sunwoo has worked in the magazine publishing

industry for twenty years, thirteen of which she dedi-cated to one company. Starting from that magazine's first issue, she's worked tirelessly for over a decade writing engaging articles, conducting interviews and overseeing photo and video shoots. After leaving her job as director of *W Korea*, Sunwoo took a two-month break (during which we played in the waters of Hawaii and Hua Hin). On her first day of work at her new job, I drove her to the office. As I watched her walk into a new chapter of her life, I wanted to stand up and give her a big round of applause. That's my diligent, lively and trustworthy retriever cohabitant!

BIKING AROUND
MANGWON-DONG

Sunwoo 'It's like once I start, I can't stop!' There was a time when I'd come home every day to a very excited Hana, telling me about how far she'd cycled that day. She would set off from home and bike to Dongjak Bridge, Seongsu Bridge, Cheongdam Bridge – going further each time. Because it was sunny, because the breeze cooled her cheeks nicely, because the clouds were drawing beautiful patterns overhead, because she was celebrating the end of a project, because our Hawaii Delivery playlist was pure purr-fec-tion! . . . Each day, she gave a different reason for why she couldn't stop pedalling. 'I thought I'd learnt how to make the most out of living in Seoul, but there's always more!' she said. Her eyes sparkled as she gushed about speeding downhill on Jamsu Bridge with the river stretching out beside her, or taking a break in the middle of the river to watch the sun retire. Hana thinks of strength training and run-ning as drab exercises that I do for the sake of keeping fit, but when it comes to cycling, she's an athlete on a record streak. Like an artist that never blames her tools, she has no complaints about riding her decade-old bike.

Before we moved, when I was just getting acquainted with Mangwon-dong, the flow of bicycles around the neighbourhood reminded me of the scenic views of Beijing and Amsterdam. Compared to my old neighbourhood, Mangwon-dong was expansive and flat, perfect for getting around on a bike. There is a market in the centre, and I'd often see ajumeonis and old halmeonis leisurely cycling home on their rusty bicycles, a bag of heavy potatoes or stalks of green onions poking out of a slightly dented basket. Watch-ing them, I got the feeling that I'd be living in this neighbourhood for a very long time. After we moved in, I would see the laundry shop ahjussis steering their bikes with one hand, a mountain of jackets and shirts covered in plastic balanced on their shoulders, on their way to deliver their customers' clothes. *This is Mangwon-dong.*

And so, when our one year anniversary of living together coincided with Hana's birthday, I figured what better gift than a brand-new bicycle? We took a taxi to the store, Hana picked her bike and I swiped my card. She was practically shaking when she ran her fingers along the sleek, black Titicaca. Without a moment's hesitation or sparing a thought for me, she hopped on to her new bike and cycled the whole way home. (Bear in mind Hana's birthday is in December, and the cold snap that year was not for the faint-hearted.)

I would've loved to ride in the breeze with Hana, but the truth was, I had a slight phobia of bikes. Like Hana's old ride, the wheels on my Mini Velo were tiny and offered zero stability, and the slightest turn of the handle would throw the bike off balance. Instead of swerving smoothly, I had to hit the brakes whenever a car came out of nowhere or the neighbourhood kids dashed towards me. Then there was that time when, on my way to get hangover soup, I'd fallen off my bike and torn open my knee. Come spring the following year, it was my turn to be gifted a new bike – for a very different reason, of course. I'd somehow managed to put off the gift-giving for a few months until Hana's persistence won over, and we went back to the same shop to buy a Titicaca like Hana's. One that I promptly folded up and loaded into the car because I didn't dare ride it back home.

The autumn I got my new bike, I became one of

those people that I'd always found 'very strange and eccentric, to be honest'. That's right, I became someone who cycled to work. As it turned out, cycling was the quickest way from our house to my office. The commute was thirty minutes by bus, and no taxi driver would accept my booking because of the short distance; but by bike, fifteen minutes was all it took. I'm just an amateur cyclist, so allow me the liberty of blaming my tools. Because once I got an upgrade, my fear of cycling vanished. I could deftly manoeuvre my way around any obstacles and go up any gentle slopes easily as long as I shifted into the seventh gear. And oh, my lovely thighs, how they proved their strength in the face of steep inclines! Why didn't I get into cycling sooner? I felt like a person who'd been sitting on a bed when she could be sprawled out on it.

When I'm driving or riding the town bus, I see the world in different frames and at different speeds. Among the countless views, the one that I see from my bicycle is the most vivid. On the way to work, the warmth of the morning sun hugs me, and at every stop sign, the cool breeze kisses my cheeks. Just the thought of getting on my bike makes me excited about going to work. I've realized now: *Ah, this is why Hana can't stop.* This is why she ends up at Cheongdam Bridge, forty whole kilometres away. Sure, there are plenty of more expensive gifts out there, but none richer in stories than a bicycle. The Han River, alleyways, great weather, firm thighs, pleasant work commutes, and our strange and eccentric selves – Hana and I have shared them all.

IF WE BROKE UP

Sunwoo   Whenever Hana and I get into a fight, there's something that I do in secret to appease my rage: I open my real estate app and go through the listings. *I'd lived alone just fine! Why suffer when we can just go our separate ways!* I'll huff, and scour for an apartment, much smaller than our home, where I could be by myself. It might happen one day. If we get into a *really* big fight, if one of us gets married, or if our trajectories part ways. I think having a few rules in place could help us prepare for that day and say our goodbyes properly, sort of like having a prenup sitting in the drawer. But that's an idea that I've kept to myself.

I suppose all the furniture would be returned to its respective owners. Hana would keep the bookshelf that her carpenter friend built, I'd keep the pretty white-framed TV and the fridge, a housewarming present from my mother, and the air purifier that

Hana's mum bought would obviously go to Hana. Now the things that we've bought together and that we've received as gifts are trickier. The table and reading chair set, the lights we shopped for together and all our oak pieces reflect our shared tastes and hold many unforgettable memories. Perhaps we'd go through each item, and it would go to whoever loves and cherishes it more. Somehow that idea stirs up the depressing image of furniture in an estate sale, each piece marked by a red 'to be auctioned' sticker.

When I'd asked Hana about her thoughts on this, she'd replied coolly: 'One of us will have to break the arrangement first, right? Either because we can't bear to live under the same roof for a minute longer, or because we've fallen madly in love with some guy. Well, whoever it is should give up their furniture rights!'

It seems Hana is confident she won't be the one to call things off. Or maybe, unlike me, she just isn't attached to material things. Anyway, in the event that one of us leaves, it's unlikely that the other will find a new replacement roommate. In the same way as when we'd bought the house, we'd probably split the sale proceeds, and look for our own places.

Whatever happens to the furniture, there's one point on which Hana and I both agree: we have to live close enough so that we can drop by anytime to see the cats. It's for the sake of both us humans and our cats. Having been a family for years now, our bond has deepened. Haku, Tigger, Goro and Young-bae have become not only precious to us, but also to each other. If humans get sad whenever they have to be apart, imagine how much worse it is for cats who cannot understand why they must be separated. We've got friends in the neighbourhood who make fine catsitters, but none of them know enough of the cats' histories to fill Hana's or my shoes. Only Hana and I know which cat has had bladder surgery, which cat plops itself down in the bathroom whenever it's thirsty and wants us to turn on the tap, which cat throws up after eating too quickly and which cat walks funny when it's constipated.

Whenever I look at the prices of the neighbouring apartments, I'm reminded of how ridiculous housing prices are, how troublesome it is to move and of all the things I'd have to repurchase, and these inconveniences lead me to the same conclusion: I should patch things up and live happily with Hana. My resolve steels every time we patch things up. 'When it's good, it's great' is what Haruki Murakami says about his married life, and the same applies to us. I don't know if I'll ever meet another person who will laugh at all my bad jokes, make up silly dance moves as we take turns sharing our favourite songs and, at the end of a rough day, tell me I'm a good person who's doing just fine. Such blessings only come once in a lifetime, don't they? And even if I were to meet someone like Hana, I doubt I'll have the endurance to go through the whole ordeal of matching their lifestyle, arguing with them, combining our furniture, throwing out the extras, fighting over my inability to throw out my things, etc. Besides all that, what would I say to our four cats who would never know why they can't see their siblings any more? I can't let that happen.

While this may all come to an end someday, I hope that day keeps getting postponed. I, for one, have no intention of forgoing my furniture rights.

OUR FAMILY AND OUR
EVEN BIGGER FAMILY

Hana   By now you've heard all about our four cats. But the truth is, there's more. We've got Guru and Mom, who live two floors down in Ari's house, and Mango, who lives with illustrator Kim Hossi. We've also got dogs – Deokhoon, who lives with my carpenter friend Yeongju, and Yaggom-ie, who lives with Hong Yewon, a doctor of traditional medicine in the neighbourhood. Their familiar faces and personalities are a stone's throw from us. Whenever a pawrent has to go on a trip, we can rely on our network of trusty petsitters. Mr Cheol-Day Star are frequent travellers, and when they're off on a longer vacation, Sunwoo and I will help to water their plants. And when we're not home, we can count on Ari or Mincheol to look after our cats. I used to drive Yeongju and Deokhoon to the vet twice a week, and the day Yewon brought home Yaggom, a shiba mix puppy, we went over to hers to fawn over him. Walk into Yeongju's pub, Barcelona, on a random evening and you'll probably find a couple of us pawrents sipping on drinks.

Speaking of neighbourhood havens, let me introduce to you my favourite cosy neighbourhood cafes, Small Coffee and Daeru Coffee. I'd once received dried lavers as a present from the owner of Small Coffee. As I savoured them with rice, I thought, *What a warm and friendly place we live in.* There was also that time when I parked in a shopping mall after dropping off Sunwoo at the restaurant we were going to. On the way out of the mall, I bumped into the couple who run Daeru Coffee. *I'm just on my way to have lasagne. Oh, we know that restaurant! It's good!* After a bit of small talk, we went on our way. While Sunwoo and I were waiting for our food, the owners of Daeru Coffee approached us. 'Here, scan this later so you can get free parking!' they said, and handed us a white receipt. The world can be so kind to us.

The six members of our family aren't isolated. Our W_2C_4 household stands as a module within a kind and loose network located in Mangwon-dong. In some ways, we're closer to and happier to see our neighbours than our blood relatives. And unbound to familial obligations, we embrace them more honestly and warmly.

A while ago, Mr Cheol called. She was on her way to work and wanted to send some potatoes and onions from her in-laws' farm by 'elevator express'. It's a system we've invented to send stuff to each other – you put the item in the elevator and send it up or down. It all started one night when I'd received a cake as a gift and wanted to share some with Mr Cheol. Not wanting to bother her when she was probably in her pyjamas getting ready for bed, I'd texted her, *Sending you something yummy by elevator. Go out and get it!* Since then we've used the elevator express to send fruits, wine, banchan and even books. After receiving Mr Cheol's text that morning, a *ding* announced the arrival of the elevator on our floor, and the doors slid open to reveal a plastic bag full of fresh produce. As per Mr Cheol's request, I shared some of it with Yeongju. Two days later, Yeongju called to say that she'd made the best Japanese curry with the potatoes and onions, and invited me over to try it. That was how the vegetables from Mr Cheol's in-laws made their way around the neighbourhood as Yeongju's delicious curry rice.

Besides Mr Cheol-Day Star, there's another couple who lives in our apartment building – Ari and

Hanseong, whom I've nicknamed AriSeong. AriSeong and I have been neighbourhood friends since back when we lived in Seochon, but before that, Ari and Sunwoo had been long-time friends. After I left TBWA Korea, Ari joined the company as a graphic design intern, which was how she met Mr Cheol. Like me, she'd seen Mr Cheol's house and fell in love. And there you have it – three households of friends living in the same apartment building. I don't have to use the elevator express with AriSeong; our apartments are aligned with only two floors between them. What we have, however, is the 'door handle service', which is a fancy way of saying we leave things at each other's door. With two cats of their own, AriSeong make the most dependable catsitters, and since they live close, we feel less guilty about calling in favours.

Last Saturday, Sunwoo and I convinced Mr Cheol to hang out with us because Day Star was on a business trip and we didn't want her to eat dinner alone. Arms swinging freely, the three of us strolled to a mandu hotpot restaurant, and went to Barcelona afterwards. Something good had happened that day, and I wanted to treat my friends to wine. In the end, everyone took turns buying bottles, and our evening grew longer and longer. Just as it was getting late, AriSeong showed up. We joined tables and ordered more wine. It was one in the morning when we decided to leave. We said goodbye to Yeongju and the five of us set off on our thirty-minute walk home. The autumnal weather was perfect, and I was riding the high of alcohol and of walking with my friends. To have friends who would rather walk together than call a cab! It felt like we were as close as old folk from a tiny village. We share curry rice, made from countryside potatoes and onions, meet up naturally at the pub after a long week and cheer each other on, take care of each other's pets and share little gifts with one another. We're writing a good chapter of our lives together. As I write this, I'm nibbling on the most savoury peanuts, courtesy of Mr Cheol's in-laws.

THE PEOPLE I SURROUND
MYSELF WITH ARE MY FAMILY

Sunwoo   Just as autumn was ending, everyone in the office received an email. All employees were entitled to a medical fee subsidy and were thus encouraged to get their flu vaccinations by November. It was a way to maintain productivity amid flu season and keep the office virus-free. The benefit was extended to family members of the same household, who were prone to infection by way of sharing the same living space. After getting my vaccination at a clinic near work, I went home with a numb arm and told Hana that I wished she could've gotten the shot, too, and that she *should've* been able to. Because even though she isn't officially registered as such, she's my family.

I have a friend who lives with her partner. Although they're not married – and have no plans to do so – they have a dog together and have combined their finances for years. One night, her partner was rushed into the ER with stabbing pains, and my friend spent several sleepless nights watching over him. When she was asked to fill in the paperwork, the limited options in the relationship section forced her to write herself down as 'friend'. The same thing happens whenever she receives registered mail on his behalf. These little instances in her everyday life muddy the identity of her relationship.

In real life, there are relationships that fall outside the conventional labels commonly found on paperwork. If I were to fall very ill or have to be rushed into surgery, it's not my mother – all the way in Busan – but my cohabitant who'll be at my side in a flash. Likewise, I'm always ready to fulfil my role as Hana's caregiver. If only there were an option that connotes greater responsibility and trust than 'friend', so that Hana and I, and my friend and her partner, could check it and be properly represented. A word like 'life companion', perhaps.

It's out of this need that the Life Partnership Act – a bill allowing cohabiting partners to receive income tax benefits, be registered as dependants under national health insurance and access medical records – is being discussed. A similar bill has already been in enacted in France. The Civil Solidarity Pact (commonly known as PACS) provides tax and welfare benefits to unmarried, cohabiting partners. In South Korea, all employees who've made a political donation can receive a small tax deduction. It's become an annual ritual of mine to give that amount to a female politician who represents and advocates for my rights. A few years ago, I donated to Jin Sun-mee, member of the Democratic Party of Korea and the woman who brought the Life Partnership Act to parliament. When asked if the bill posed a threat to the existing family structure, Jin said, 'The existing family structure is not put at risk by any particular bill, but by harsh realities that make looking after one's family members impossible. The Life Partnership Act is here to empower families by giving them the ability to look after one another.'

Single households are growing, and will only continue to do so. The way people live evolves faster than any law, institution or concept. Just as workers are no longer devoting themselves to one company until retirement, people are starting to break out of the traditional obligations of blood or marriage. Besides, we live in an age where the average life expectancy is inching towards one hundred. As the population of unmarried couples, divorcees and widowed spouses ages accordingly, there will be more people, like Hana and me, looking to turn to their friends for companionship.

If so, where should welfare policies go from here? My hope is that we're heading towards cohabiting partners and kindred spirits being given ample support to properly fulfil the role of each other's legal guardians.

To devote one's life to another by marriage is a beautiful thing. But so is the labour of looking after someone during a particular season of life. If notwithstanding blood and marital ties, individuals are willing to devote themselves to caring for others, it is only right that they are well supported by laws and institutions. As family structures become healthier, stronger and more diverse, the aggregate happiness of the society they form is bound to increase, too.

FIVE YEARS LATER, WHAT
HAVE WE BEEN UP TO?

Hana   When *Two Women Living Together* was published in South Korea in 2019, it became a hot topic and was warmly received. It was as if our society had been waiting for a book like this. But it wasn't just South Korea, the book has since been translated into many languages and sold to territories like Japan, Taiwan and China. Sunwoo and I have given many interviews and done several photoshoots, including a fashion shoot inspired by our life for *SPUR Magazine* in Japan. With the royalties and the money we earned from book promotions, we were able to pay off our mortgage. The permanent shadow drawn across Sunwoo's face has lifted at last, revealing a smile befitting a woman of the sun.

The year this book was published, Sunwoo and I were invited to libraries and bookstores all over the country. We gave book talks and, while we were at it, had ourselves a vacation. The people who came to our talks were from all walks of life, but they showered us with the same blessings: *Always be happy! We're rooting for your molecule family!* You would think we were newlyweds. We spoke in the most unexpected places – Muji, 29CM, the Hyatt – and even received an invitation from the justices at the Seoul Central District Court. There, after hearing all about our lives, someone came up to me during the refreshment break and kindly offered some advice. 'You never know . . . If there comes a time when you have to divide your assets, even a handwritten document could be put into effect.' Sunwoo and I have got into several huge fights since, but I haven't had to take that advice, thankfully. If we hadn't written this book (and unless we'd committed a crime or landed ourselves in trouble), we would've never had the opportunity to visit the Seoul Central District Court. *Two Women Living Together* has opened a whole portal of unexpected opportunities.

Sunwoo has since quit her office job to work freelance. She has published a book of interviews titled *You're an Unni if You're Cool,* an essay collection on work called *You'll Die Doing Your Best* and a compilation of her letters to and from author Kim Honbi titled *The Courage to Say I Love You.* Meanwhile,

I've published an essay collection titled *Talking about Speaking*, another on reading classic literature called *Golden Bell Sound*, and I also co-wrote *Victory Note* with author and mother Lee Okseon. One day, Sunwoo came to me with an interesting proposal. We'd received an invitation from the tourism board of Queensland, Australia, and she suggested that we write a book about our travels. I agreed immediately, thrilled by the thought of exploring Australia for the first time together. The trip didn't disappoint. But just as we were about to publish our manuscript, the Covid-19 pandemic hit, and the publication date was postponed. It wasn't until May 2022 that *Sister Trip to Queensland: Two Women Travelling Together* was published.

That's right – Sunwoo and I braved the pandemic together. With all our activities cancelled, we stayed in, smothered by depressing news. During that time, we suffered a sudden heartbreak: Goro, our second eldest, passed away. The following year, I lost my father. At the funeral, Sunwoo, my father's best drinking buddy and honorary son-in-law, broke down before his funeral portrait. With each loss, we sunk deeper into shock, sadness and depression. Looking back, those were some of our darkest hours. Yet we saw them through, because we had each other. Haku was diagnosed with chronic kidney disease, and every day since, we've made sure to administer her daily injection and medicine. When we first rushed into buying a house and introduced our cats, these incidents had lived only in our minds as vague futures. Life is fraught with pain and loss. But as my cohabitant and I overcome heartaches and emotional whirlwinds, I know that our relationship will toughen. There are so many things I'm grateful to her for.

After its publication, there were more and more opportunities for Sunwoo and I to work together as the two women in *Two Women Living Together*. As well as book talks and interviews, we moderated movie screening discussions and recorded an audiobook. Behind a mic, our voices blended well together, and our conversations flowed naturally. In April 2022, we started our podcast, *Two Women Talk*. As of 2024, we've recorded more than a hundred episodes and come tomorrow, we'll probably be chatting into our mics, recording the next episode. Our listeners, whom we call Toctoros – a portmanteau of our favourite Ghibli character, Totoro, and the word 'talk' – are our biggest supporters; the ones holding a giant leaf above our heads when it rains.

Our neighbourhood friends are doing well. Since 2022, Sunwoo and I have teamed up with two other friends to start the MPC aka the Mangwon Ping Pong Club. Although we meet twice a week, our ping pong skills have yet to improve. Our thighs and friendship, however, have firmed up. After hours of running and sweating, we always treat ourselves to a delicious lunch. Sunwoo and Mr Cheol are taking pottery lessons. At first I doubted Sunwoo's butterfingers would be any good at sculpting plates, but I've been told that her teacher thinks she's got the chops. Judging by the photos Sunwoo shows me, I suppose it's true. Here's a secret: whenever I gush over her creations, I think, *Good! Now you can break your own plates.*

Sunwoo and I are living happily as drinking buddies, conversation partners, workout mates, co-pawrents and professional colleagues who trust and take responsibility for each other. If one of us has to focus on writing or falls ill, the other will step in to do the chores or look after them, a kindness that will be remembered and duly repaid. This arrangement has proven much more effective and helpful than when we lived alone and stretched ourselves thin. We may be a long way from the Life Partnership Act, but outside of marriage and familial ties, DIY families like ours will only continue to grow in number.

On 19 July 2024, our interview was published in the *New York Times*. We were surprised to see not only our photo, but also a very striking head-line: 'As Many South Koreans Shun Marriage, Two Women Try to Redefine Family'. The article touched upon the success of the book and our podcast, and introduced us as two South Korean women defy-ing traditional familial structures and amplifying women's voices. They mentioned my struggle with Sunwoo's 'natural-disaster-sized' wardrobe, which I found surreal and too funny. We're a *New York Times*-featured DIY family! The journalist, who'd been covering alternative familial structures in South Korea, told us that it was our dear readers who had recommended our book. I'd like to thank our readers for loving this book, and for helping our message travel. Us two women will do our best to live happily together.

SAYING GOODBYE TO GORO

Sunwoo   People who don't know cats well often mistake their *meow*s for crying. Actually, *meow* is how they strike up a conversation and *meow?* is their way of saying hi. Sometimes, they'll even shriek, *Eomma! Unni! Aw, whyyyy?* Since her eighteenth birthday, our firstborn Haku has gotten into the habit of waking up the whole house with an ear-splitting *woooaaaak!* We hear her loud and clear: *I'm starving! Where's my food?!* Twice a day, we'll mix her medicine and supplements into her wet prescription food, and each time, we'll change up the ingredients slightly to appeal to her appetite. Picky about everything down to her feeding bowl, Haku will take one sniff and saunter away if her food isn't perfectly placed in the centre of a flat, wide plate. Like gourmet chefs, Hana and I will carefully mash up tuna or chicken with a spoon, plate it nicely and top it off with a splash of scallop broth. Still, there are times when Haku would huff, *This is so not it*, and we'd sag in defeat. In those times, we'll squeeze a bit of puree on top of her food or crush up a crunchy treat and transfer everything to a new plate. You might find more cat bowls than human plates in our sink. This is what living with senior cats looks like – dedicating all my time and labour to my furry children.

As we enter our eighth year of living together, Hana and I are now approaching our late forties, and our cats are ageing faster than ever. Haku is eighteen, Tigger is fifteen and our youngest, Youngbae, is thirteen. In human years, they're grannies in their eighties. Nothing hurts more than knowing that your cats are old and sick. That sadness hits the hardest when we get asked about our travel plans. Whenever we tell our friends that we can't travel at the same time because someone has to give Haku her daily injection, they sigh and say, 'It must be difficult.' If I weren't a cat owner, perhaps I would also pity us; perhaps I'd live never knowing that even in sickness, there is joy and laughter. Youngbae can never keep still unless it's time for her asthma medication. Holding her in my arms while I wait patiently for her to breathe in her cough medicine brings me peace and a sense of fulfilment. Sometimes I wonder if the satisfaction of taking care of our cats comes from losing Goro.

Goro's sudden death was the most tragic incident that Hana and I had to overcome. I mean, what were the chances of us coming home from a work trip, excited to cuddle our cats, and finding one of them dead? When the catsitter came the night before, he'd been just fine ... Every now and then, the memory of finding Goro lying completely still resurfaces and trickles down my cheeks. We wrapped his body in a blanket and rushed him to the twenty-four-hour vet. He'd always been a chubby cat, but in that moment, his stiffness weighed heavier in my arms. I knew Goro couldn't be brought back, but I had to know why he died. In a tear-choked voice, I asked for an autopsy. *He was perfectly fine before. How could this happen?* With a sympathetic expression, the assistant at the desk explained that they couldn't do anything more for a dead animal, and suggested that we look into a pet funeral service. Thinking back, she was just doing her job. I must've looked deranged. Why did I behave that way? Why did I make such an absurd request? I suppose I simply couldn't accept that Goro was gone. Four years have passed, and still I choke up at this memory; still I blame myself for not doing anything for him.

In the Q&A segment of our live podcast show celebrating our second anniversary, a Toctoro asked: *I was a cat mom of two, until my youngest passed away very suddenly. The both of you have been through something similar with Goro, how do you cope when you miss him . . .?* My breath hitched in my throat and the rest of the question blurred out. But it was up to me to answer the question. Crybaby Hana was already weeping.

'We miss him terribly. Whether it's a person or furry friend, the death of a family member can leave a big hole in our lives. No matter how much time passes, their absence lingers, and not a moment goes by without you wishing they were still here. When I miss Goro, I give my other cats a hug. It's not the same as hugging Goro, I know. Just like how no two humans are the same, our cats have different bodies, coats, temperaments and souls.'

After Goro's passing, I started seeing things – a big, chubby cat sitting beside the sink, by the front door, inside the tub . . . There were times when I didn't dare part the shower curtains. After some time, the visions stopped. Now I catch glimpses of Goro in Youngbae's face. Especially when Youngbae is grooming herself while lying down or resting splayed out on the floor. Perhaps it's because Youngbae is gaining weight in her old age. But I know it's all in my mind. I see Goro in corners of the house, in

our other cats, in the dogs walking past, in the float-
ing clouds and in the field of flowers because my
heart yearns to see him. In these moments, I always
feel a bit sad. Yet the thought that Goro is all around
us fills me with warmth and peace.

Haku has lost over a kilogram and barely weighs
two kilograms. Due to severe canker sores, she drools
nonstop, leaving both her body and corners of the
house with a foul scent. But she's alive, and the way
she shrieks for food both annoys me and reminds me
of her strength. I wonder: *Isn't loving a living thing
essentially staying by their side as they grow weaker,
sicker and eventually die?* I didn't know this eighteen
years ago, when I brought baby Haku into my life.
Each passing day has taught me that to live with a different species is to bid the slowest farewell. But for
now, Haku is still with us.

A happy life isn't achieved by preparing for and
avoiding pain, loss and agony. Without those, perhaps
life wouldn't be life at all. Had I known about the diffi-
culties of watching my cats grow old and sick, and the
pain of saying goodbye, would I have given up the life
that Haku and I have built together? But the moments
before the farewell, the moments when we love with
every fibre of our being, the memories that rekindle
a loved one's peculiarity, and those that sometimes

bring us pain – aren't those the pieces that make up the fabric of life?

'Shortly after saying goodbye to Goro, our lives were oppressed by a heavy and profound sense of loss. While the sadness has dissipated, it hasn't disappeared. I think it will continue to live with us. But isn't its presence proof that we'd met a very special creature? That we'd lived a life no one else has . . . one that is only ours to cherish.' While the recorder outro played, Hana and I used the clean side of Haku's hanky to wipe off our tears and snot.

There's a hole in Hana's and my heart. They are the same shape, that of a big and handsome cat. They represent our pain, our loss and our happy memories.

They mark the spot from which we loved.

THE BIRTH OF SEOUL CYBER MUSIC UNIVERSITY

Hana   As a gift for graduating elementary school, my parents bought me an acoustic guitar. I tried to teach myself by following the handbook, but after many failed attempts, I pestered my parents for guitar lessons. 'Music school? What for!' they said in their thick Busan accent, and brushed me off. Throughout middle and high school, I slowly taught myself. Studying the scores in music books like *Pocket Pop Songs*, I'd hum the melody to myself while I strummed chord after chord, I could never get the F chord to sound right because of my small hands, but I enjoyed playing guitar alone. After graduating high school, I came to Seoul; I left behind my guitar and grew further away from playing instruments.

Stuck in the office late one night, I went online and bought a bass guitar. I couldn't stand the thought of wasting another day away in the office without a hobby, and what better way to get rid of stress than spending money? I've always been drawn to guitars, and of the different types, I was particularly fond of the deep timbre of bass guitars. At last the sleek instrument arrived at my door and, with my hard-earned adult money, I signed up for lessons. But then I ran into two problems: one, on days when I had classes, I had to lug the heavy instrument all the way to the office and then on to the bus heading towards Jongno. Two – and this was the bigger issue – I was too short to wear a bass guitar across my body. I was longer horizontally than vertically, which rendered a pathetic image. Pressing on the strings was a whole other problem. In the end, I gave the instrument to Mr Cheol-Day Star and said goodbye to my bass guitarist dreams.

Once I became a freelancer, I was free from the shackles of a nine to five and had more time to spare. Around then was when I met the instrument that I'd stick with for a long time. It was part of the guitar family and came in a size much less imposing than a bass guitar – the ukelele. In the springtime when the afternoon sun prickles my back, I like to sit by the window and play, filling the room with the ukelele's carefree and languid twang. The petite instrument suits my small frame and hands. It's perfect for me.

One day, I asked Sunwoo if she knew how to play any instruments, or if there was one that she would like to learn. We must've been chatting with our Hawaii Delivery playlist playing in the background. Music has always been an important part of our lives. Anyway, Sunwoo said, 'I think I'd like to have a go at a wind instrument like the clarinet. When I was a kid, I loved playing my recorder.' I made a mental note and, when Christmas came, I surprised her with a gift. Thinking that a clarinet might be too big and expensive, I'd opted for something more subtle: a recorder. The night before Christmas, I snuck it into her red stocking, and during breakfast the next day, I hinted, 'Looks like there's something in there.' Sunwoo lit up when she saw the recorder, and launched into a sequence of songs.

Sunwoo was born to blow a flute! She looked like a pied piper out of an old fairytale, bewitching the villagers with the trill of her recorder. Granted, her repertoire consisted purely of old cartoon theme songs, but every note rang accurate and clear. As I watched her put on a solo Christmas concert, playing song after song without sheet music, I thought, *To think I almost went my whole life not knowing the musical genius hidden inside her!* It seemed Sunwoo's body remembered the recorder from her elementary school days. That was my proudest Christmas.

But perhaps that two-hour concert had drained her artistic soul completely. Or maybe she just got tired of the instrument's sound. Because for a year after that, Sunwoo didn't pick up her recorder at all. At the end of the year when *Two Women Living Together* was first published, I chanced upon an amateur choir perform-ance which invigorated the performer in me. I slung on my ukelele and asked Sunwoo to grab her recorder. Sunwoo played the melody to 'Rudolph the Red-nosed Reindeer', 'White Christmas' and 'Silver Bells' while I backed her up with chords. Sunwoo and I stared at each other wide-eyed – we were making music and we sounded *good*! Our instruments were basic, practic-ally children's toys, but together, they created a lively harmony rich in texture. I realized it then: *All my life I've been waiting for the melody to my accompaniment.* Riding the high, I made an Instagram post:

Hana, Sunwoo and their four cats present the Mangwon-dong Bremen Live Band! Catch us on Instagram Live at 6.30 p.m. tomorrow, Christmas Eve. Hear three Christmas hits performed on ukelele and recorder . . . Blink, and you might miss it! (Literally. Because we don't know many songs hehe.)

Our Instagram Live performance was a huge success. Surprised by how good we were, our audience cheered for us in the chat. Someone suggested that we name our band the 'Seoul Cyber Music University', a parody of Seoul Cyber University's jingle that goes, 'My era of success begins at Seoul Cyber University!' It was the perfect band name – we lived in Seoul and performed online. And thus, the Seoul Cyber Music University, or SCMU, was born.

After our debut performance, we played more online shows and grew slowly as a band. But what really launched our music career was the Covid-19 pandemic. Stuck at home during the lockdown, we spent more time with each other and our instruments, and let out our frustrations through music. I suppose the latter counted for something, as the SCMU had never sounded better. Our setlist grew as we added more complex pop songs like Red Velvet's 'Peek-A-Boo', and no song was too complicated or fast for us. When social distancing measures were lifted, the SCMU were invited to play offline shows. Our first performance was in Chekbang Oneul in Yangjae-dong, where we opened for a book talk. Later, at author Kim Honbi's book talk for *You'll Die Doing Your Best*, she joined us on stage with her moktak, a wooden percussion instrument used by Buddhist monks, and the three of us would do many other shows as a trio. Kuldiga, a bookstore specializing in classical music, suggested that we give the classics a try, and we performed pieces by Chopin, Elgar and Haydn. When our podcast *Two Women Talk* held a special live show called *Toctoro Together*, we performed in front of five hundred Toctoros and received a warm round of applause.

This year, Sunwoo started to learn the flute. It seemed she was ready to move on to something with a wider range of notes, something that provided a challenge. As the patron who'd awakened the musical genius in Sunwoo with my Christmas gift, I took it upon myself to buy her a music book holder and flute stand.

An ensemble is a wordless conversation. Whenever Sunwoo and I play a song, the exchange between our instruments creates a symphony. Good conversations expand worlds. A lover of classical music, Sunwoo once took me to see an orchestra. I was blown away by how beautiful the wind instruments sounded! I wondered if it was the exposure to Sunwoo's music that allowed my ears to recognize the beauty of the winds. A while ago, while listening to Kim Hyeoncheol's 'Train to Chuncheon', I'd picked up on the familiar cadence of the flute playing in the background. How had I never noticed it before? I'd known the song since I started learning the guitar on my *Pocket Pop Songs*! Some beauties lie dormant inside of us until a good conversation comes along and prods them awake. I hope our conversations on music play on for ever. Our era of success begins at SCMU!

TWO WOMEN TALK

Sunwoo   Good conversations anchor us – living with Hana taught me this. Trivial conversations about how many kilos I lifted at the gym, how our money plant and monstera are growing and when we should make that gangdoenjang recipe we found ground us to our daily lives. But good conversations can also take us places – to revisit literature or music from centuries ago, to the inner workings of a brilliant mind, to unfamiliar places, and even to the future to witness the flow of societal change and catch a glimpse of our silver-haired selves. Though we might be at home, our conversations are sails that will take us far. 'Since all we do is talk in the living room, why don't we put a mic on the table and hit record?' With that, we started our podcast, *Two Women Talk*.

Before *Two Women Talk*, Hana hosted Yes24's bookish podcast *'Chek' It Out*. For four years, she interviewed authors and pampered bookworms with the latest book recommendations. When the podcast ended, I was sad to see Hana's eloquence go to waste, but more than that, I missed listening to her stories and craved more. And so I suggested we start our own independent podcast. Since the release of *Two Women Living Together*, Hana and I have done countless book talks, interviews and miscellaneous promotional activities, all of which have made me confident in our work synergy. Then, at the beginning of 2022, we got the big push we needed to start. Monika and LipJ, two dancers from the survival show *Street Woman Fighter*, were cast in the reality TV programme *DIY Family*. The two were members of the same dance crew, Proudman, and like Hana and me, have been living together for years. Before the show was broadcast, the producers called us to explain that they were creating a show focusing on found families, and asked for permission to name their show after the phrase 'DIY family', which they'd come across in our book. Imagine our surprise when we turned on the TV to see LipJ recommending our book to the world! This is our moment! Now's our chance! We named our podcast and recorded our first two episodes, 'DIY Family? Here's Where it All Started' and 'Being in Your Forties Isn't So Bad'.

Our channel flourished like cucumbers after the

monsoon. Two months after uploading weekly episodes, we were contacted by representatives from
three of the biggest podcast platforms, Podbbang,
Apple Podcasts and Spotify. Our skyrocketing sub-
scriber count had caught their attention and they were
keen to work together on future collaborations. *Two
Women Talk* ranked number one on the Apple Podcasts Popular Chart, joining in the ranks of podcasts
produced by major broadcasting stations like MBC,
JoongAng Ilbo, TBS and Content Lab Vivo. Whenever
I recall seeing our little thumbnail amid the logos of
big name companies, my chest swells with pride. I'd
been recognized for my accomplishments and efforts
at work, of course, but this was different. Building
this little podcast from scratch and then launching it
into space to shine among the stars made me feel . . .
a strange sense of security. It was an assurance that
came from knowing that it wasn't money or the back-
ing of any big company but our strengths and skills
that had got us here, and that the latter was what will
ensure that our future will be all right. On our own,
Hana and I are lacking in many ways, but together,
there's nothing we can't do. I don't know how else to
describe it. It's like we're a quaint family restaurant
that has received a Michelin star.

Just as we've divided the cleaning and cooking,

Hana and I have different roles as producers. We plan and record our episodes together, but Hana handles the tech stuff and editing and I'm in charge of our PR. We've got different fortes – if we're two people on a boat, I'm the muscle rowing the oar, and Hana's the captain peering through her binoculars and deciding where we'll go. Our synergy isn't born out of hard work, but something else – perhaps something closer to fate or good fortune. 'How do you maintain such a good working relationship?' Whenever we get this question, we say, 'The most dangerous/worst attitude you can have in a working relationship is, "I can do what she does." You have to think, "I can never do what she does. Thank God for a capable partner!"' Just the thought of spending an entire day copy and pasting audio clips makes me depressed. On the flipside, the thought of answering emails, phone calls and texts and playing Tetris with our meeting schedules stresses Hana out.

The motto of our podcast is, 'If you see something good, talk about it.' We're not cheery because life has been easy and beautiful. In fact it's the opposite – it is precisely because, as we grow older, we see more of the world's ugliness and meet more cynics and pessimists that we're intent on staying positive. In a world where nothing is absolutely good or bad, we want to focus our finite energy on talking about, remembering and documenting the good things that deserve more attention. Our motto has created a powerful magnetic force. Two years after starting the podcast, we've recorded more than a hundred episodes, and more significantly, have surrounded ourselves with like-minded Toctoros. We built a small house, not knowing that our neighbours would fill our courtyard with good food and music, and that we'd have ourselves a banquet. Women in their twenties and thirties tell us we've given them the courage to live the lives they want. Since a woman in her forties introduced her sixty-year-old mother to the podcast, their conversations have taken on so much colour. Kids who listen to the podcast with their mothers send us letters, drawings and bubbly voice recordings. Groups of Koreans are forming Toctoro groups all across the world. The women CEOs of small brands that we advertise on our podcast have a group chat where they can connect with one another. The Toctoro universe grows bigger and stronger.

'Don't Sweat it', 'Talk Yourself Up, Let Yourself Feel Down', 'Be Meddlesome', 'Work it, Ladies', 'Life Is AMF (Art, Music and Fitness)', 'Being in Your Forties Isn't So Bad', 'Take That Licence Out of the Drawer' ... The messages that we send by way of podcast episodes are spoken with one genuine hope: that instead of exhausting themselves trying to check society's stifling boxes, women will love and embrace their authentic selves, and dare to explore new ways of living. Because that is how Hana and I would like to live. On top of manuscript deadlines, lectures and book talks, Hana and I record every Sunday and upload every Tuesday. There are times when the loaded routine suffocates me, but in those moments, I remind myself that *Two Women Talk* is the dream that Hana and I are still working towards, and I get back on the mic – for the dream that our conversations will touch hearts, spark ideas and thoughts, and help us all see the world through brand-new eyes.

About the Authors

Kim Hana, originally from Busan, moved to Seoul at the age of nineteen and has lived in a variety of housing arrangements. Living with Hwang Sunwoo, she simultaneously experienced unprecedented stability and big life challenges. Hosting a podcast for Korea's largest online bookstore, she has shared a variety of books and authors with the general public and is the author of several books herself.

Hwang Sunwoo, also from Busan, started living alone in Seoul at the age of eighteen. While she loves her independence, living with Kim Hana quickly blossomed into a fully-fledged family with the two of them and their four cats. She has worked as a features director for the fashion magazine *W Korea* for many years and has published essays and interviews on various topics.

Kim Hana and Hwang Sunwoo live together in Seoul. They co-host a weekly Korean-language podcast, *Two Women Talking Together*, and have also published a music playlist book, *Hawaii Delivery*.